SUCCULENT GARDENING

A Beginner's Guide to Growing Succulent Plants Indoors and Outdoors

By Jacob Wells

SUCCULENT GARDENING

© Copyright 2020 - All rights reserved.

The content contained within this book may not be reproduced, duplicated or transmitted without direct written permission from the author or the publisher.

Under no circumstances will any blame or legal responsibility be held against the publisher, or author, for any damages, reparation, or monetary loss due to the information contained within this book. Either directly or indirectly.

Legal Notice:

This book is copyright protected. This book is only for personal use. You cannot amend, distribute, sell, use, quote or paraphrase any part, or the content within this book, without the consent of the author or publisher.

Disclaimer Notice:

Please note the information contained within this document is for educational and entertainment purposes only. All effort has been executed to present accurate, up to date, and reliable, complete information. No warranties of any kind are declared or implied. Readers acknowledge that the author is not engaging in the rendering of legal, financial, medical or professional advice. The content within this book has been derived from various sources. Please consult a licensed professional before attempting any techniques outlined in this book.

SUCCULENT GARDENING

By reading this document, the reader agrees that under no circumstances is the author responsible for any losses, direct or indirect, which are incurred as a result of the use of information contained within this document, including, but not limited to, — errors, omissions, or inaccuracies.

SUCCULENT GARDENING

Table of Contents

Introduction V

Chapter One - The Origin Of Succulents 1

Chapter Two - Types Of Succulents.................................... 18

Chapter Three - How To Grow Succulents Indoors 35

Chapter Four - How To Grow Succulents Outdoors 70

Chapter Five - Caring For Succulent Plants..................... 98

Chapter Six - Fun Facts About Succulents 128

Final Words 138

INTRODUCTION

If you are somebody with an interest in the world of gardening, then you probably noticed that there has been a recent spike of interest in a couple trendy topics lately: the first is the rise of cannabis cultivation, which has taken off as the restrictive laws around growing have begun to change; likewise, there has been a major push for more indoor and organic gardening, as more and more people want to escape the world of GMO and chemically induced fruits and vegetables. Both of these trends interact with a third trend: hydroponic gardening, also known as soilless gardening, which uses flowing water to provide nutrients. Chances are, however, that you haven't heard much about the fourth trend that has been rising as of the last couple years: growing succulents.

Google search trend data shows a steady increase in the number of people searching for information about growing their own succulent plants. However, unlike with flowers, fruits, vegetables, or herbs, there is a large portion of the general public that doesn't know what a succulent is. When they hear the word "succulent," their first thought is as a description of a juicy steak or a box of expensive chocolates. In actuality, **succulents** are a category of plant defined by the way they suck up and store water inside their leaves. They take their name from the Latin word for juice (or sap), *sucus*.

There are many different kinds of succulents, ranging from caucuses, to aloe vera and the "black rose" zwartkop plant. Even the dragon fruit comes from a succulent cactus. Many succulents are edible and provide nutritional health benefits, while others (such as aloe) are used in treating burns or cuts. There is a large range of succulents grown for an even larger variety of reasons. But in the same way that reasons to grow them vary, they also vary vastly in how difficult they are to grow. Many succulents can be quite easy to grow, and are perfectly content to take care of themselves rather than having you tend to them. However, some can have exacting requirements that take a lot of attention and tender care. What this means for the casual gardener is that there are plenty of succulents they can start growing to learn the ropes, along with many more they can tackle later once they feel more comfortable working with succulents.

Succulents have a tendency to prefer dry climates, which is why they evolved to store water within their leaves rather than using it all up at once. If you compare them to an orange tree, for example, you see that the orange tree requires a lot of water because it uses it all to produce fruit. Most succulents don't produce any fruit (the dragon fruit plant being an exception to the rule), so they are free to store their water to survive through long stretches of dry weather. In this manner, succulents are kind of like the plant version of a hibernating bear—bears eat lots of food while they are awake so they can store fat in their stomach and survive off that fat during their hibernation period. Succulents do something similar, but with water instead of fat. However, although succulent plants can survive a long time without water, just like the bear will still need to eat, succulent plants will still need to be watered if they are to stay healthy.

The goal of this book is to introduce you to the wonderful world of succulent gardening and provide you with enough information to get started raising your own healthy succulent plants. In order to achieve this goal, this book will follow a straightforward path that assumes you have little to no knowledge on how to take care of these fascinating plants. Chapter one explores the origin of succulent plants and where they come from, how their biology works, and why they make such great additions to your indoor or outdoor garden. Chapter two will introduce some of the popular succulent plants to you, which may want to grow; these will be divided between those succulents that thrive indoors and those that prefer being outside. Continuing to follow this division between indoor and outdoor succulents, chapter three and chapter four will look at the requirements for growing indoor and outdoor succulents respectively. Chapter five will bring these two threads back together and look at how you care for and maintain your succulent plants, so they stay healthy and pest-free. Finally, chapter six will focus on fun and interesting facts, along with additional advice that may not fit in anywhere else.

By the time you put the book down, you will be able to get your hands dirty planting your own succulents and enjoying the many benefits of these wondrous plants. So what are you waiting for? It's time to get growing.

CHAPTER ONE

THE ORIGIN OF SUCCULENTS

Succulents are a growing craze, with many people being exposed to their beauty through social media sites like Instagram. But these intriguing plants don't literally come from the internet, of course—to find out where succulents come from, you need to take a much wider lens. In fact, you need a *global* lens to answer that question, as succulents can be found all across the world, though the most well known areas that succulents spawn are in dryer climates such as the Africa, India, the deserts of North America, and the rainforests of South America. Succulents are strong plants that can survive weather that is far too harsh for other plants, such as climates with high temperature and little rain. Despite these specific climates, there are still plenty of succulents to be found along oceanic coasts and lakeshores.

Since succulents are truly a plant variety that could be described as global, we won't spend much time focusing on the geographical origin of these plants. We will touch on it briefly, of course, but that will be when we look at specific kinds of succulents, such as aloe vera or zebra plants. To locate succulents as a whole on a geographical scale would be a fruitless exercise, but on the individual species level, we will have a much easier time. So, rather than worrying about each succulent's geographical origin, let us look at the evolutionary origin of these fascinating plants. You will see why their origin has consumed the minds of many biologists, their being truly as unique and intriguing as they are beautiful.

Succulence and the Two Kinds of Succulent Plants

SUCCULENT GARDENING

The first step to getting to know these plants is to understand what succulence is. The agreed upon definition for **succulence** is the way that water is stored within the plants' cells; specifically, the way that water is stored within cells that are still alive. Succulence, as a process, depends on various factors, ranging from the volume of the plant's cells to how they fit together on a microscopic level, along with how thick their cell tissue is. Because these parameters are all prone to change from plant to plant, and especially between different species of succulents, succulence should be considered with a wider scope than, for example, photosynthesis. Because the definition of succulence is so wide, you could actually argue that most plants are technically succulent; however, the category of plant species that we call *succulence* can be separated from other plants because of the amount of succulence they undergo and the way in which they make use of the water stored in this manner.

The comparison to a hibernating animal is an apt one for describing the purpose of succulence. Plants of the succulent variety store water inside their leaves so they can survive in arid or dry conditions. While most plants suck in water through their roots and put it to work immediately, succulents conserve water and think ahead to when they will need that water next. Upwards to 90% of a succulents leaves are actually composed of water, but there are different kinds of succulents that are divided because of the way they store water. **Storage**

succulents have a tissue called **hydrenchyma**, which is an achlorophyllous water-storage tissue. Other succulents merely store water within chlorenchyma cells, which stores chloroplasts that help with photosynthesis. Succulents that store water within the chlorenchyma are called **all-cell succulents**, since the water is stored within the plentiful cells rather than specialized ones like hydrenchyma. Storage succulents tend to be *perennial*—plants that survive all year—so they would use their water to make it through droughts. All-cell succulents are more often annual plants, and they use the water they store to increase the length of time they can grow.

Despite how many may think of succulents as exclusively growing in arid and dry areas, this thought is merely a misconception. Succulents don't actually grow in abundance in these environments; rather, succulents prefer to live in areas that are semi-arid. This means that while these environments are still very dry, it is not surprising to have rainfall within them. Succulents store water; they cannot make it themselves, so the most arid environments could not provide them with enough H_2O naturally to live. Again, consider a hibernating animal—these creatures don't live in winter conditions all year round, but instead, they store nutrients throughout a good chunk of the year, then go hibernate. Succulents can be thought of as hibernating more than they are out gathering nutrients, but they still need rainfall to gather the necessary resources to survive their hibernation.

SUCCULENT GARDENING

How Do Succulents Interact with Their Environment?

The organs involved in succulence do more than just store water. In fact, there are whole fields of study that focus on the understanding of how the interaction between succulent and environment is different than the interaction between non-succulent plants and their environment. Processes that are simple for many plants, such as transpiration, are completely different in plants of the succulent variety. Understanding how succulents interact with their environment is important for those who wish to add them to their garden because knowing what may be good for a tomato plant, for example, may actually be quite damaging for a succulent plant.

The size of the succulent organs in a plant, together with the density therein and how much water is being stored at any given time, all contribute to the overall temperature of a succulent plant. The physical structures of most succulent plants prevent them from being able to take in or let go of water through transpiration, so these plants had to learn how to withstand their leaves and stems being left at temperatures higher than most other plants can endure. The succulent organs give these plants a high thermal capacity, which not only allows them to withstand more heat, but it also prevents them from losing all that heat at night; a fluctuation that would otherwise be quite damaging to a plant's health. All this contributes to allowing succulents to exist in very warm conditions. On the flipside, most succulents cannot deal with low temperatures, and freezing damage can easily kill a plant in a short amount of time.

Since succulents primarily store water within their leaves, they are known for having much thicker leaves when compared to other plant species. Because of this thickness, it is much harder for light to penetrate through to the middle of a succulent's leaves. This lack of penetrative ability is made less extreme by the environments that succulents favor, as these are often areas with lots of light and little foliage to shade smaller plants, which would include succulents. While the middle of a succulent's leaves are hard to reach, the same cannot be said about the rest of the succulent's body. Once again taking into account the high levels of light in their preferred environments, the amount of light that succulents are exposed to would be considered worrisome for other plants and often would be enough to cause sunburn or death to them. Succulents have evolved several techniques to lessen the effects of this light exposure. If you look closely at the different varieties of succulents, you will notice how many of them have hairs on their leaves, an outer coating of epicuticular wax, a surface of powdery content, or many different little spines. These are defensive adaptations designed to allow the plants to strive in their semi-arid environments.

Succulents that make strong use of photosynthetic processes have cellular structures that are tightly packed together with only a quarter as many spaces for air molecules to pass through compared to other kinds of plants. What this does is restrict the rate of photosynthetic processes in succulent plants and reduce the thickness of leaves in succulents of the all-cell variety. The cellular structures of storage succulents, on the other hand, are often not quite as densely packed. Both types of succulent plants have species with far more stomata than other plant types, which are tiny openings on the surface of the leaves that allow for gas to enter or leave more readily. This helps to offset some of the constrictions that arise from such tightly packed cellular structures.

Why Are Succulents Growing in Popularity?

We have seen that succulents come from semi-arid environments within which they have evolved to survive, so we could consider the question of their origin to be answered. However, one question that this evolution does not answer is why succulents have seen a recent rise in popularity. It isn't like they are something new—they have been around for between five to ten million years, and the aloe vera plant was used by ancient Egyptians for medicine and beauty as far back as six thousand years ago. Extant writings recovered from the ancient Egyptians indicated that the aloe vera plant was considered a sacred plant that held the secrets of immortality. While this isn't true (at least, not as far as we have discovered yet), it does tell us that humans have had a relationship with succulents for as long as we have had the ability to record history. So, why exactly is a type of plant we have known about for millennia just *now* catching everybody's interest?

The answer to that question is found in two places: the first is the plant itself; the second is the technological developments we've made within the last twenty-five years. Let's begin with the plant.

One of the biggest factors in the popularity of succulents is the fact that they are so easily maintained. Unlike most plants found in a typical indoor garden, succulents don't need to be transplanted into a larger pot as they grow. A succulent will take the first pot given to it and call it home. Therefore, if you have purchased a fancy new pot, there is no harm in transplanting your succulent to it; it is an aesthetic choice rather than a maintenance one. Succulents also don't need to be watered very often, which means they don't eat up as much of a gardener's schedule when compared to most other plants. This reduced watering schedule also means there is a reduction in problems with pests, as many pests are drawn to moisture, meaning that they would be more inclined to go after plants that are watered on a more regular basis. Succulents also grow very slowly, which alleviates the need for regular pruning. The fact that they grow so slowly also means there is no need to worry about them getting too big to be kept indoors. All of these characteristics make succulents an excellent choice for people with little to no experience with gardening.

SUCCULENT GARDENING

However, there is one more attribute that makes these plants such a compelling purchase: they are beautiful. Succulents come in all different shapes, sizes, and colors, which makes them very attractive. No matter where you want to put a succulent, there is going to be one that perfectly accentuates any yard or room. It is because of how beautiful these plants are that they are getting so popular, as their beauty directly ties into the role that technology has had in popularizing them.

With the invention of the internet, people all over the world finally had a platform on which to share photos and connect. As social networking has grown in the last decade, the bigger player after Facebook has been Instagram; a photo sharing network that has more than a million active users in the United States alone. When you factor in the rest of the world, this number is drastically higher. It has been through Instagram that succulents have really taken off and caught the public's attention. This comes back to their beauty. These are very photogenic plants and images of them constantly get a ton of interaction from people when they are posted. Because of their beauty, they have grown more and more desirable over the last few years.

So, technology and beauty have brought succulents to the attention of the world, but they wouldn't have taken off it wasn't for how easy they are to maintain. If they were horribly demanding plants, only a handful of people with a real itch to get their hands dirty gardening would bother to raise them for their aesthetic appeal. The fact that these absolutely gorgeous plants are low maintenance makes them the perfect combination for public consumption; yet, this still doesn't fully explain their popularity, for that there is one final piece to the puzzle: health benefits.

The movement towards sustainable living, eco-friendly lifestyles, and organically grown products has risen in popularity alongside succulents. This is fortuitous timing, as these movements have seen a rise in interest for alternative medicines and sources of nutritional value. As it just so happens, succulents are great sources for both of these interests. Looking at the health benefits of just a couple types of succulents reveals this to be the case. The leaves of the opuntia plant are a great source of fiber and calcium, while their fruit is packed with vitamin C. Both the leaves and the fruit of the opuntia plant are low in calories as well. Sea beans, or the salicornia plant, can be eaten raw or fried up with some spices to serve as a source that is high in protein, iron, iodine, and calcium. The aloe vera plant helps reduce the pain of scrapes, burns and rashes but it can also be a bit of a superfood with over 75 phytochemicals, tons of antioxidants, vitamin C, vitamin E, folic acid and three different B vitamins. Plus, there have been studies linking consumption of aloe to constipation relief. That's only a few. There are around sixty different plant families that have some type of succulent in them, and many families have more than one (like the Orchidaceae family for example, which includes acampe, aerangis, ansellia, bolusiella, bulbophyllum, cirrhopetalum, calanthe, cyrtorchis, eulophia, liparis, oberonia, oeceoclades, polystachya, tridactyle, and, most famously, vanilla).

It is the combination of beauty, ease of maintenance, and health benefits, alongside the rise of social networking, that makes up the driving force behind the newfound popularity of succulents. In a lot of ways, we are only just starting to properly appreciate these plants like the ancient Egyptians did so many many millennia ago.

The Future of Succulents

While this chapter primarily set out to trace the origin of both the biological and social evolution of the succulent, an interesting note about their future arose during the researching stage of the project. Global warming has been affecting many plant species, and environmental issues have become hot button topics in the last few years, rightfully and depressingly so. One result of this environmental phenomena has been a call for more succulents to be planted and tended for.

This is because of the succulence process itself. While water levels are set to rise and this topic takes up a lot of press time when it comes to discussing global warming, there is also a rise in droughts that has begun to occur and is projected to continue rising. Droughts are scary things to a farmer of traditional crops like carrots, lettuce, tomatoes, oranges, or strawberries, but to the succulent farmer, a drought is nothing to worry about. Since succulents store water for use through dry periods, they are the perfect fix to this particular problem. Plus, while many succulents aren't worth eating, there are many that will still provide enough nutritional value to replace these more traditional staples of our meals.

It could just so happen that succulents provide the answer to how humanity will deal with global warming's disastrous effect on global farming practices. In some ways, it suggests that perhaps the ancient Egyptians were right to see plants like the aloe vera as sacred. They may just be what will allow us humans to survive the looming environmental and ecological crises that we are facing today.

SUCCULENT GARDENING

Chapter Summary

- Succulents tend to come from dry climates such as Africa, India, or the American deserts; however, these plants can be found all across the globe and can even survive along the shores of both oceans and lakes.

- Succulence refers to the way that water is stored inside of living cells, though how this process happens depends on the volume of the plant's cells, the thickness of the tissue, and their arrangement on a cellular level.

- Many plants actually make use of a kind of succulence, but to a far lesser degree than those that we have labelled as succulents.

- 90% of the leaves of a succulent plant are comprised of water, which is done to conserve and store H_2O, so the succulent can survive long periods without rain.

- There are two types of succulent plants: the first is called storage succulents, and these conserve water through a specialized tissue called hydrenchyma, which serves as an achlorophyllous water-storage. The other type are called all-cell succulents because they store water within their chlorenchyma cells rather than any specialized type.

SUCCULENT GARDENING

- All-cell succulents are more often annual plants that use stored water to extend the length of their growing period, while storage succulents are more often perennials that use their stored water to survive droughts.

- Succulents most naturally grow in areas that are semi-arid, rather than completely dry places. These semi-arid locations still see the rare rainfall, but it is this rare rainfall that provides the succulents with water to store and use, so they can survive to see the next rare rainfall. In this manner, the life of a wild succulent is a continuous cycle.

- The succulent organs of these plants help them to regulate their temperature. The increased thermal capacity that these organs provide allows the plants to withstand higher temperatures and keep their temperature from undergoing extreme drops during the night. However, temperatures around 90°F will still damage the plants, and low temperatures will cause freezing damage that can kill them quickly.

- The leaves of a succulent plant are quite thick because they are filled with water, which prevents light from penetrating them fully. However, light can still easily hit the rest of the succulent plant's body, which would normally leave a plant at risk of burning. Many succulents have developed defense mechanisms to prevent this occurrence, such as an outer coating of epicuticular wax or tiny hairs that cover the leaves.

- Succulents with heavy photosynthetic processes have tightly packed cellular structures that would normally slow down or stop these processes. In order to compensate for this, all-cell succulents have smaller leaves. Both all-cell and storage succulents have more stomata on their leaves (small little openings) to let gas escape easier.

- Succulents have been gaining popularity because of the intersection between the rise of social media sites like Instagram, their beautiful aesthetic, the ease with which they are maintained, and their many health or nutritional benefits.

- There has been a call to grow more succulents that have nutritional value as the processes of storing water can allow them to survive major droughts that have been and will continue to kill more traditional crops each and every year.

In the next chapter, you will learn all about various different succulent plants that enjoy living both indoors and outdoors. Among the indoor succulents that will be covered are popular species like aloe vera or panda plants. Outdoor succulents will include varieties such as the aeonium or stonecrop plants. This chapter will also look at the key differences between growing succulents indoors or outdoors, so you have a better understanding of why you would want to choose one above the other.

CHAPTER TWO

TYPES OF SUCCULENTS

As has been previously mentioned, we will be focusing on the categorization of succulents that are best grown indoors and those that prefer the outdoors. In many ways, this categorization is arbitrary; all succulents are technically outdoor succulents in the same way that all plants are technically outdoor plants. They are naturally a part of nature, and to bring them indoors is in and of itself an unnatural act.

However, for the purposes of education and structure, this division serves us well. You more than likely already know whether you are looking to grow indoors or out, so this allows you to read what is important to your situation and skip what isn't. In continuing with the education side of it, it also allows us to look at all the options available to us and get as much detail on the topic as is possible in a single book.

SUCCULENT GARDENING

This chapter foregoes the worries of gardening itself and, instead, narrows its focus down onto the plants. While it isn't feasible to look at all possible succulent plants (it isn't even possible to look at all the *families* that have succulents in them), this overview will cover a lot of ground and should give you a well-rounded idea of the variety of succulents available to start growing today.

Growing Succulents Indoors vs Outdoors

As was previously mentioned, succulents are plants, which mean they naturally grow outdoors. As it turns out, this simple fact is also the strongest argument that is made for growing succulents outdoors rather than inside. The argument for growing succulents outdoors is further supported by how these little plants are notoriously tough, coming up in some of the worst environments. However, they do really enjoy their dry climates, so long as the temperature doesn't go above 90°F for too long at a time. If the temperature in your area is often 90°F or greater for long periods, then your succulents are best kept indoors to avoid burning them. To circumvent this, growers who plant succulents in containers like to either bring them indoors or move them to shaded areas during the summer.

What about for people who don't live in warm, dry places? Places that are especially wet or cold can also cause stunted growth or death in succulents, as they will overly gorge themselves on the water or may have difficulty adapting to the cold. On the other hand, the dry conditions inside your house are probably quite ideal for these little guys. Another key reason that succulents have increased in popularity lately is precisely this: they have no problem hanging out on your desk and keeping you company while they grow. You can be sure to protect them from extreme fluctuations in temperature or humidity because you are able to control the climate of your house and there are fewer pests to bother them.

Of course, growing succulents indoors has its own challenges. Providing enough sun can be difficult if there are obstructions blocking the sunlight from coming in your windows throughout the day. This can be compensated for by purchasing grow lights, but doing so could jack up the cost to maintain your plants, as well as how much time and effort must be given over to their care. The speed that indoor soil dries out is also different from soil outdoors, and it is important to keep in mind these facts when reading advice about growing succulents, as many articles found online speak about growing them outdoors without making reference to this fact. Essentially, much of the information available will make the assumption that you are growing *outdoors*, which can lead the indoor gardener to accidentally mistreat their succulents.

The division of succulents into indoor and outdoor varieties is based on several components: The first is the extremity of temperatures and climate that the plants like. While most succulents don't want to be too warm, there are those rare exceptions that prefer to be practically burning, and it isn't feasible to keep the temperature as high as your plants would want indoors. By contrast, there are many succulents that *won't* take to the climate in your area naturally, so it has to be artificially provided by bringing them indoors to protect them from the elements. You will notice that the majority of indoor succulents are green plants, and this fact isn't just a coincidence. Succulents that are primarily green have an easier time photosynthesizing and can handle indoor conditions much easier than brightly colored purple or red plants, which have a tendency to require extra care to survive indoors while naturally flourishing outside.

It should be noted, however, that despite this division into indoors and outdoors, you can always go against what has been suggested and choose to plant an indoor plant outdoors. There is nothing stopping you from making this decision; just make sure you take your local climate and the plant's needs into account before you do so. If you happen to live in the type of climate that the plant favors, then growing it outdoors will make just as much sense as growing it indoors. However, if your local climate doesn't fit the plant's needs, that does not mean that your plant will die when you plant it outdoors. Succulents are quite strong and able to resist adverse conditions fairly well, but using the energy necessary to put up this resistance will mean that your plants grow much slower. That's also if they grow at all, since adverse conditions can easily stunt their growth. Always, *always* do your research, so you can provide your succulents with the best possible care.

Indoor Succulents

Panda Plant (kalanchoe tomentosa): This succulent never grows very big at all. Most succulents in general are usually on the small side, but the panda plant is *tiny*, even by succulent standards. At first glance, you may think that the leaves of the panda plant are white and red; however, on closer inspection, you will notice that the leaves are green but covered in fuzzy white hairs, like a coat of fur. The ends of the leaves are decorated with red dots, whose color pops brightly against the white hairs, and the combination of red and white coloring reminds one of a red panda. Panda plants can actually flower in its natural habitat, but it is exceedingly rare for one to do so when raised indoors. If you are lucky enough to see your panda plant flower, you will see that they are a beautiful yellow and green mixture in the shape of little bells.

SUCCULENT GARDENING

The panda plant lives for quite a few years, which means that you can expect to be looking after it for some time. This shouldn't be a problem, however, considering how easy it is to take care of this little guy. It enjoys bright light and it doesn't need to be watered too often, preferring for the soil to completely dry between drinks. You don't need to worry about the humidity level around the panda plant either, so long as the room it is kept in is an average humidity. If you are growing an indoor garden that uses a humidifier to alter the natural levels of the space, you will want to keep your panda plant in a separate location. You may want to move your panda plant outside during the warmer months, in a space with shade. This is entirely optional, of course. What *isn't* optional is the fertilizing of your panda plant, which should happen once a month during the warmer season. A panda plant should be fertilized with a NPK balanced fertilizer, which simply means a fertilizer with an even ratio of nitrogen (N), phosphorus (P), and potassium (K).

Aloe Vera (aloe vera): One of the most well known of all the succulents, the aloe vera plant has one of the most fascinating stories in history. There are records of its use dating as far back as 6,000 years in ancient Egypt, as we've covered, but that is only scratching the surface of its story. We also have records placing the aloe vera plant in ancient Mesopotamia, traditional Chinese medicine, India, and by Native Americans before colonialism in the Americas. It even finds its way into the hands of some of the most well-known figures in history; like Alexander the Great, who used the juice from the plant to treat the wounds of his soldiers, and Christopher Columbus, who grew the plant aboard his ships to aid with healing.

The aloe vera plant's relationship with healing has only continued into the modern day, with various gels being made from its juice to treat cuts and burns. While the plant itself is quite plain to look at, with an appearance best described as "spikey grass," its many medicinal uses make it an excellent plant to grow yourself. Plus, you shouldn't forget that it is jam-packed with antioxidants and vitamins, making it a great addition to your diet. To add it to your diet, simply remove the tough outer leaf and blend the inner leaf into shakes, or chop it up to add to your home cooked dishes. As far as maintenance goes, keep your aloe vera plants at a temperature between 55°F and 80°F, and only water it after the two inches of the soil has dried out (roughly once a month in the warm months and even less often throughout the cold ones). Fertilize once a month or less with a NPK balanced solution and provide it with bright but indirect sunlight.

Zebra Plant (haworthia fasciata): Much like the panda plant, the zebra plant is a succulent named for having an appearance that may remind one of an animal; this time, it has the black and white stripes of a zebra. The zebra plant is made up of green vertical leaves with horizontal white variegated stripes. While it lacks the black of the zebra, the raised stripes cast a small shadow that makes the green of the leaves look almost black. These plants only grow to around five in a half inches in both height and length, which makes them easy to store anywhere around your house. Just make sure that the location they are stored in has plenty of bright light, while again avoiding direct sunlight.

SUCCULENT GARDENING

Since the roots of the zebra plant don't extend very far, these little guys only need the smallest of containers to call a home. They flower once a year, typically in late August, though the flowers can last between one to six weeks, depending on the variety of zebra plant and environmental factors. It is the first of the indoor succulents looked at in this book that really loves being watered. The soil of the zebra plant should never be allowed to fully dry out, and the plant benefits from being misted with water often through the warmer months. Smaller zebra plants need a temperature above 60°F, while larger ones can't stand anything below 70°F. Zebra plants should be fed a NPK balanced liquid fertilizer on a weekly basis during the growing season, reducing down to once every three or four weeks during the colder months of the year. A desire for high humidity allows the zebra plant to feel at home in most indoor fruit and vegetable gardens, despite not offering much nutrition itself.

Pincushion Cactus (mammillaria crinita): It might sound strange to hear, but there is quite a heated debate within the world of botany about whether or not cacti are a type of succulent. Some voices argue that they are, whereas others argue that they comprise an entirely independent category all on their own. However, if we use the process of succulence described in chapter one as our metric, then cacti are definitely a form of succulent, and the pincushion cactus is a particularly beautiful one at that. The pincushion cactus is named for the hundreds of tiny spikes that cover it. Indeed, many people call to mind an image similar to that of the pincushion cactus. What they probably don't envision is the beautiful pink flowers that crown the heads of these cacti, nor is it likely that they picture a cactus so small, as these little guys only grow to about six inches or so.

The pincushion cactus needs to be planted in a soil with lots of drainage, and the soil should be left to dry out between watering. Where many succulents require a reduced watering schedule during the winter, the pincushion cactus foregoes any watering during the colder months of the year as it enters into a dormant state until spring. These cacti should be kept at a temperature no lower than 50°F and no higher than 75°F, which is a large enough window to allow the pincushion cactus to be tended for alongside quite a range of other plants. The beautiful flowers of the pincushion cactus bloom in the spring when temperature and water demands are met. Forgo watering these cacti for the first few weeks of spring to increase the chances of flowering and provide it once a week with a fertilizer blended for cacti to further increase your chances.

Outdoor Succulents

Stonecrop (sedum spp.): The stonecrop is a succulent that comes in all sorts of different colors. Often green though sometimes silver, blue, or pink, this oddly shaped plant is composed of circular tubes with little nubs on the top that give it the appearance of fingers. They grow rather tall for a succulent, ranging between one to three feet in height. During the summer, the stonecrop's fingers open up into flowers that appear more like leaves than petals. One of the edible succulents, the stonecrop has a bitter flavor, almost like pepper, that can add a kick to salads. The bitterness can be reduced by first sauteing the leaves. If the leaves are red when they flower, it can be eaten raw, while yellow leaves are slightly toxic and need to be cooked to compensate for this. People eat this plant primarily because it is believed to be a naturally occuring cough suppressant and has been shown to lower blood pressure. The stonecrop plant also has medicinal value beyond consumption, as it can be used like aloe vera to treat burns.

These plants enjoy lots of sun, even directly at times, though they should be given shade during the hottest months of the year. If the temperature drops beneath 50°F, then the stonecrop will go dormant. For the best growth, keep a stonecrop plant between 50°F and 70°F throughout the winter and 70°F to 85°F during the summer. These succulents are particularly resistant to the effects of drought and, as such, they only need to be watered infrequently when young. Older stonecrop plants don't need to be watered at all, so long as they have not recently been transplanted. When watering, water the soil directly and avoid wetting the plant itself.

If you are using soil with plenty of compost, then there will be no need to fertilize the plant, but if you do need to, then a weaker liquid fertilizer is recommended. There is no reason to prune a stonecrop plant except to alter the direction of growth for reasons of space or aesthetics, which should only be done after the stonecrop has finished flowering.

Zwartkop (aeonium arboreum): There are many different kinds of aeoniums beyond just the zwartkop, and we'll look at another here in a moment. The zwartkop is a favorite of growers around the world due to its beautiful, dark purple color. It is this color and the way that the zwartkop's petals open outward from the middle that has given it the nickname, "the black rose." This color comes out during nearly three quarters of the year, but the winter weather brings out a whole different side of the zwartkop. During the coldest season of the year, the zwartkop flowers a bright yellow, which couldn't be any further away in tone from its typical, black rose appearance. This purple color is a clear indication that the zwartkop should be planted outdoors, preferably in full sun. Another reason they are best grown outdoors is their tendency to grow in clusters; rarely do you find a lone zwartkop. Read about sunbursts for more information on growing aeoniums.

Sunburst (aeonium davidbramwellii): If the general rule of thumb is that green succulents are indoor succulents and colorful succulents are for the outdoor gardens, then the sunburst aeonium is the exception to the rule. This beautiful succulent grows leaves out in a pinwheel-like fashion, each subsequent vertical layer of leaves rests on the foundation of those in the layer below it, much the same way that the layers of a pyramid do. The leaves of the sunburst plant are made up of three different colors: a dark green takes up most of the center of the leaf from the base to the tip; the rest of the leaf's mass is a lighter green or sometimes even entirely yellow color that makes the dark green really stand out; finally, the edges of the leaf are a bright red or pink color that looks like someone took a highlighter and outlined the sunburst's leaves. Little rosettes bloom into gorgeous white flowers in the summer season, making the sunburst a gorgeous succulent, whether in bloom or not.

There are roughly 35 different species of aeonium, with the zwartkop and the sunburst serving as only an introduction. Most varieties are just as gorgeous in their own way, like the atropurpureum (aeonium arboreum), with its bright maroon leaves or the aeonium garnet, which looks like a zwartkop if its leaves were red rather than dark purple. Despite the variety in appearance, the care guide for aeoniums is remarkably consistent across species. Aeoniums are succulents, which don't actually enjoy hot or dry conditions. Their dormant phase, if it triggers, comes in the summer, and they can survive without the need for watering (unless it is a particularly dry period). If exposed to too much heat, the leaves of the aeonium will begin to curl up, and you may confuse the behavior for wilting. What is actually happening is that the aeonium is changing its shape to make it harder for water to escape. Still, it is best to grow them in a shaded area that will receive plenty of moisture. While summer is their dormant period, their growing season is actually in the winter. This is because the perfect temperature for growing aeoniums is between 65°F and 75°F. Despite enjoying moisture, too much will cause them to rot, so the top two inches of the soil they are planted in should be left to dry before watering.

Aeoniums make for a beautiful addition to any yard and, when properly positioned, they really don't require much maintenance at all. Of course, you could make the decision to grow them indoors, but doing so will make for a much more difficult experience. If you are new to growing succulents, you will want to get some experience with easier-to-grow species indoors before moving up to aeoniums. Still, when you are ready to start tackling harder plants indoors, then aeoniums make a great stepping stone into intermediate difficulty.

SUCCULENT GARDENING

Chapter Summary

- Succulents grow naturally outdoors, which is the main reason people suggest outdoor growing over indoor. Since succulents are also naturally tough, they can withstand a lot of environmental abuse and can grow in many areas that don't match their desired climate. However, a mismatched climate will leave a succulent's growth stunted.

- Succulents enjoy dry climates but a temperature above 90°F for long periods of time will cause them harm. Succulents tend to grow best when placed in partial shade rather than left exposed to direct sunlight.

- The dry conditions indoors are quite favorable to succulents and, so long as you can provide them with enough light and prevent extreme fluctuations in temperature or humidity, they should do fine.

- Indoor growing may require the purchasing of grow lights, which could eat up money to purchase, then even more money for the electricity to keep them running. They also eat up more of your time, as you need to be mindful of turning them off or on.

- Some succulents enjoy odd climates and lots of heat, making outdoor growing a must. However, growing succulents indoors will allow you to create an ideal climate for them without relying on the whims of mother nature. Indoor succulents also tend towards green, photosynthesizing plants, whereas outdoor succulents are more varied in their color. A good rule of thumb is to assume that colorful succulents will demand more complex maintenance routines when compared to green succulents.

- Just because one kind of succulent is listed as an indoor plant in this book does not mean it has to be. Research the ideal climate for each kind of succulent that you are thinking about growing to see if they will flourish in your local environment or not. Ones that do can be planted outside and those that don't can be raised indoors in an artificial environment.

In the next chapter, you will learn how to grow your own succulents indoors. From the container you plant them in to the location you raise them, from the soil you home them in to the fertilizer you feed them, you will learn everything you need to tend for your own gorgeous and healthy indoor garden full of succulents.

CHAPTER THREE

HOW TO GROW SUCCULENTS INDOORS

Now we turn our attention from learning about succulents to actually growing them. We'll start with those green, indoor succulents in this chapter and move to the more colorful, outdoor succulents in the next. There will be a few pieces of information that will carry over between indoor and outdoor, but we will be covering all the necessary information in each chapter regardless. This is done so if you are interested in growing only indoors or only outdoors, you will be able to find all the necessary information in either chapter rather than having to flip between chapters to learn everything you need.

Since we're starting with indoor succulents, the first step is to choose the variety that you would like to grow.

SUCCULENT GARDENING

Along with those looked at in the last chapter, some great succulents to grow indoors are also burro's tail (sedum morganianum), the crown of thorns (euphorbia milii), the flaming katy (kalanchoe blossfeldiana), jade plant (crassula ovata), roseum (sedum spurium), and the snake plant (sansevieria trifasciata). Regardless of which plant you go with, remember that the most important part in growing any new species of plant (be it a fruit, vegetable or succulent) is to research the plant's specific needs. Most succulents we will look at will share very similar requirements, allowing us to look at them generally for the most part; however, there will always be those that zig when the majority zag, as it were. Take the lessons you learn in this chapter, apply them as the general template for growing succulents, and adjust them only as is required by the specific plant you choose.

While succulents won't need as much time or attention as an indoor vegetable garden would, they are still going to have their own needs. Proper light, water, soil, containers, and fertilizer are all necessary components for growing healthy succulents. You will also want to get your hands on some gloves and hand tools, like a pair of shears or a spade. However, you shouldn't need to worry about equipment like fans or humidifiers, which are necessary for growing vegetables indoors but may be overkill when raising succulents. While used less often with succulents, you may also want to get either an electronic pH reader or a pH test kit. When first starting out, it can be tough to find the right

SUCCULENT GARDENING

balance of nutrients for your plants, and a pH reader will help you to properly fine-tune your soil and fertilizer.

We'll start this chapter out by first looking at the best containers for our succulents. These will ultimately be the spaces that our succulents call home, and it is important to provide a space that fits the needs of your plants rather than merely shoving your succulents into whatever is closest to you. Following this, we will turn our attention to the soil that fills up our containers and look around our houses to figure out the best location for our containers and, thereby, our succulents. Finally, we will explore how to make our own liquid fertilizer for use with succulent plants and learn more about how people are split on whether or not indoor succulents should be fertilized or not. With all this knowledge under your belt, you will be ready to start growing your own indoor succulents in no time.

SUCCULENT GARDENING

Picking the Right Container

When it comes to the containers that we grow our succulents in, the old adage, "one size fits all," couldn't be further from the truth. Neither is there equivalence between the different materials used to make a container. It should also be noted that not every container has the proper drainage system built in to serve as a good home for your succulents. It is these three features (material, size, and water retention) that need to be compared and contrasted when choosing a container, so you give your succulents a home that they can thrive in. To give too small of a container would be like housing a five-person family in a trailer; it might be able to fit technically, but it is going to be a tight fit that leads to plenty of problems as it grows. Let's first consider the many different options available to us for material.

SUCCULENT GARDENING

The two most popular materials used for succulent containers are terracotta and plastic. **Terracotta** is a porous material that offers plenty of breathability to the plants that are grown in it. This feature is good for many plants, including succulents, but if you live in an area that is especially hot or dry during the summer, this breathability can actually be harmful for your succulents. Terracotta containers also require more watering than other materials for this reason. Also, keep in mind that terracotta absorbs heat from the sun, so if it is left in direct sunlight, it can become very hot. While this means it may burn you, the bigger risk is that it will damage the roots of your succulents. For these reasons, terracotta is best used in partial shade and in areas that are naturally humid.

Terracotta containers can also end up being a little pricey and very heavy when filled with soil. This makes them the opposite of **plastic** containers, which are traditionally quite lightweight and inexpensive. The lower cost makes plastic containers the go-to choice for many growers all over the world. If you purchase a succulent from the store, chances are good that it came in a plastic container. Plastic doesn't breathe very well, so it holds onto water and moisture much more effectively than terracotta does. Their light weight also makes it easy to check how much water your succulents have in their pots, as all you need to do is lift up the container and check its weight. Chances are good that first-time growers will be raising their succulents in plastic, as this reduces the cost to start.

Another material that is commonly used to make containers for growing plants is ceramic. **Ceramic** containers come in *glazed* and *unglazed* varieties. Unglazed ceramic is pretty similar to terracotta in make, but it isn't able to breathe quite as well because the type of clay used to make it is very fine grain. This means that the spaces between each molecule after the firing process are much tighter. Unglazed ceramic holds moisture in pretty well, which means that if you go with unglazed ceramic, you won't need to water the succulents in those containers as often. On the other hand, glazed ceramic is actually quite a bit different from both unglazed and terracotta. These pots have a layer added to them to give them the glazed look. You can tell the difference immediately, as glazed ceramic containers have a shine to them that is indicative of this extra process during their manufacture. This extra layer may make glazed ceramic look really pretty, but it also makes them unbreathable. Glazed ceramics can still be used for growing succulents, but if you decide to go with them, you need to be extra vigilant about checking the soil prior to watering, as it is easier to overwater succulents in a glazed ceramic container compared to those a more breathable material. Also note that while porcelain is a different material, it can be linked to glazed ceramic as it functions almost identically.

SUCCULENT GARDENING

Other options include glass, concrete, resin, or wood. **Resin** pots are pretty much just another form of plastic, though they are often shaped into more interesting and weird designs than plastic is. Resin also tends not to look like resin or plastic, with many finishes hiding the fact that they are made of resin unless touched. **Glass** containers, on the other hand, function like glazed ceramic does, though these don't often have drainage holes built in (a feature that we'll be looking at in more depth in just a moment). Because of the lack of drainage holes, glass containers are most often used as terrariums but the risk of overwatering your succulents is even higher than it is with glazed ceramic, as glazed ceramic is more likely to have holes for draining built in prior to purchase. **Concrete** planters are fun to make yourselves and can be painted into all sorts of pretty colors, but they are best used for smaller plants because the weight of a concrete container grows exponentially with size. Concrete should be shaped to have drainage holes but, overall, concrete has very poor breathability and can be a major pain to work with. **Wood** containers are also an option, but these are best used for outdoor gardens rather than indoors. Wood is also damaged by water, so a layer of waterproofing needs to be put in place prior to adding any soil. Wood also rots over time, which leaves wooden containers requiring extra maintenance when compared with other containers.

If you have never grown anything before, then stick with either a plastic, terracotta, or unglazed ceramic pot for your first succulent. Each of these will require different watering schedules, but they should provide your succulents with quick enough drainage to prevent any moisture damage, so long as you don't water them too much. Always, always check before watering. Also note that there are more factors to a good container than just the material; we will next have to turn our attention to the size.

When it comes to containers for your succulents, bigger doesn't always mean better. In fact, bigger might actually be the *worst* choice for your succulents. The reason you would want to have a large container for a plant isn't because the top part of the plant with its leaves and stem. These are the most visible part of any plant and they might take up a lot of space, but the real reason for a large container is the part of the plant that you don't see: its roots. Plants with long root systems require larger, deeper containers, so the roots don't all get tangled up and stunted.

Succulents, however, tend to have really short root systems. These don't need much space at all, so all the extra depth of the container is only going to go to waste. But what's worse is that the extra soil in a large container is only going to keep the moisture trapped in for longer, doubly so if the container is made of a material that doesn't breathe. This is dangerous for a succulent, as too much moisture in a container can promote rot. While you can still plant a shallow rooted succulent in a large pot, it will take extra steps to keep it safe. You are better off going with a shallow pot to fit your succulent's shallow roots. Remember to keep in mind that there are some succulents, the Haworthia to name one, that have long root systems. There are exceptions to every rule, but it tends to be a safe bet to match your succulents to smaller pots.

Regardless of size, your chosen pots should always have drainage holes. Although not every container will have drainage holes (and some may not technically need them), it is best to keep it safe and make it a rule for yourself to use only containers that have them when growing succulents. A lack of drainage hole won't necessarily kill your plant, but it will make it doubly important to be careful when it comes to watering or fertilizing your succulents. Drainage holes allow water and moisture to escape from the container. This means that your succulents are given the chance to dry out, which is more in tune to their natural environment. When it comes to succulents, it is better to err on the side of dryness rather than wetness. Too much moisture will cause rot, so the best way to combat this possibility is to use a container with drainage holes and a potting mixture that drains quickly.

So with that, you now understand the three key components you need to consider when picking a container for your succulents. You need to balance drainage holes and breathability, while picking a size that reflects the needs of your succulent rather than just what looks the best. Keep in mind that there are limitless shapes, sizes, and colors when it comes to garden pots, and you can always paint them yourself if you want. Even plain pots can be a great fit for a succulent when you consider how beautiful these plants are on their own. Whatever you choose, first make sure it is the right fit for your plant before worrying about how it fits your house.

The Right Soil for Indoor Succulents

When it comes to soil, it benefits us growers to take an active role in making our own potting mix. While you can go to any garden center and ask for a prepackaged potting mixture for your succulents, you are inherently giving up a level of control when you do so. While the package will tell you what is supposed to be in it, it doesn't necessarily follow that the packaging will be correct. You may end up with a mixture that is off balance or made from poor ingredients. While this fluctuation is unlikely to kill your succulents, it does make for a second-rate mixture. Most of these mixtures have a tendency to drain poorly as well, and this can increase the risk of rot.

Rather than go with a commercial potting mixture, why not make your own? You can take full control over the soil you home your plants in to ensure maximum comfort. This also allows you to fine-tune issues of drainage, which is a huge plus since too much moisture is the biggest threat to your succulents. And the best part? It is easy to do and will save you money in the long run. To make your own succulent soil, you will need three ingredients.

The first ingredient to a good succulent soil is an **all-purpose potting soil**. You don't want to use heavy garden soils or even a potting mixture, but rather stick with an all-purpose soil such as those used for indoor plants. Some gardeners will swear by certain brand names, saying that they're the only soil they trust; although, it doesn't really matter which brand you go with, so long as it offers a plain potting soil. Look for what is on sale at your local garden center and go with that. Just make sure it doesn't have *vermiculite* added in, as they might add it to soil to hold onto moisture longer; we are looking to have the exact opposite effect.

The second ingredient is **coarse sand**. This can be replaced with turface or poultry grit, but this ingredient is important to help make sure that the soil mixture drains quickly and your succulents don't ever have to worry about rotting. While you could just go to the beach and fill up a bucket with sand, doing so may be a bad idea for the same reason we use all-purpose potting soil rather than just dig for dirt from your backyard. We can't control what germs or pollutants are in the sand from the beach or the soil from your backyard. It is better to purchase the raw ingredients and mix it together; that way, you know the quality of your ingredients. We want to provide our succulents with a high quality mixture, after all. Look for the type of sand that they would sell for use in sandboxes.

The third and final ingredient is to add perlite to the mixture. Perlite will further help amend your soil and give it better drainage. It really cannot be stressed enough just how important it is that your succulents aren't overwatered or exposed to too much moisture. **Perlite** are small, white, rock-like pieces that are added to many potting mixtures. If you look at a bag of premixed potting mixture and see little white specs, those are almost definitely perlite. Perlite doesn't hold onto moisture very well, and it helps to prevent the soil

SUCCULENT GARDENING

from getting too compact. What this means is that there will be more room for the soil to breathe and drain.

With your raw materials purchased, you will also want to get a **trowel**—a container to measure out your ingredients in—and another container to mix them all together. Once you have everything ready, it is time to start mixing.

Measure out three parts potting soil, two parts coarse sand, and one part perlite. Since parts is a loose term, just make sure that whatever you designated as a *part* is what you use for all the rest. If you are filling up a bucket as a part, then use the same-sized bucket for each. Likewise, if you are using a scoop as a part, then keep it consistent. When it comes to mixing a succulent soil, the important aspect is the ratio of ingredients used rather than the exact size or amount.

Once you have all your parts prepared, you have already made it through the hardest part of the mixture. The only thing left to do at this stage is to toss all your measured ingredients into the container you have set aside for mixing and stir it all together. You can use your trowel here, but you could even mix it by hand, so long as you washed and dried your hands properly ahead of time. Keep mixing up the soil until all three parts are spread out evenly. You'll want to mix it until you can no longer separate it back out by hand. Once this has happened, you now have a succulent potting mixture.

SUCCULENT GARDENING

Fill up the containers you will be growing your succulents in, so there is only an inch to half an inch or less between the top of the soil and the top of the pot. Once you have filled up your containers, they are now ready for succulents to be added.

Since you purchased the raw supplies necessary to make your own succulent mixture, there is a good chance that you had enough to mix up a large batch. If you find yourself with more succulent soil than you have use for, you don't need to worry about disposing of it. Your homemade succulent soil can easily be stored for later use. This actually makes it a pretty good idea to mix up a large batch to store and use for later plants; that way, you only have to mix up another one when it has all run out. Simply throw any remaining soil into a large bucket with an air-tight lid to keep pests out. Store this bucket in a dry location and only pull it out when you need more succulent soil.

There you have it—you have now made your own succulent soil. This fast-drying soil can be used for more than just succulents; just ensure that whatever you plant with it prefers quick draining rather than holding onto moisture.

Where to Grow Your Succulents Inside

When it comes to where you should grow your succulents, the invention of modern day electricity provides indoor gardeners with plenty of choices. Your succulents will want a certain amount of sun every day, but thanks to grow lights, this no longer has to come from the sun itself. The light your succulents need can be entirely provided through artificial means if the requirement arises. Keep in mind that the needs of your plants will need to be tailored based on what each particular species of succulent requires, but a general rule of thumb is to ensure that your succulents get no less than six hours of sunlight a day.

This is done easiest by growing your succulents on a window sill. As long as there aren't any buildings or foliage blocking the rays of the sun, a window sill would make a perfect home for your potted succulents. Your best bet is to go with a window that faces either the south or the west, that way your plants get as much sun as is possible. If you have to choose between multiple windows, take a day or two and keep track of how much sunlight each receives. Set your succulents up in the section that has the most light. A minimum of six hours is required, but your succulents will do better with even more.

If, for whatever reason, you don't have a window that provides six hours of sunlight, you will need to purchase an **electric grow light**. These come in many shapes and sizes, but if you are only growing one or two succulents, you won't need something overly expensive or powerful. Sticking with LED lights designed for use with plants is a smart choice because they don't take up much power and they last for a ridiculously long time. If you need to use a grow light, you will want to set a schedule for turning it off and on, perhaps turning it on in the morning before work and off again in the evening when you return. It is always best to create a schedule ahead of time, so you know exactly how much time and attention you need to give to your succulents care.

Keep in mind that setting your succulents up in a window with plenty of sunlight doesn't mean you don't have to keep an eye on them anymore. If you are living in a particularly hot area, you should be keeping watch of your succulents to make sure that they aren't being burned. If you notice that the leaves of your plants are burning, it is too hot where they are. You may want to consider moving them to another window sill that receives less light, therefore staying cooler, or you may want to purchase a sheer curtain, which will offer partial shade and will bring the heat down a little bit. Experiment with what works best for your budget and for your succulents.

If your succulents aren't receiving enough light then you may notice that they grow upwards in a thin manner. Spindly plants like this are a sign that they need more light. You might also notice that the succulent begins to grow quite thin as they stretch out toward the light. For example, if you have it on a shaded window sill, you might notice the leaves stretching out toward the rays of direct sunlight. These tell you that you need to provide them with more light, and they are as clear a clue that you need to adjust your plants. Always check with your plants to see how they are looking, so you know exactly what you need to provide them with.

Also keep in mind that you don't necessarily need to grow your succulents on a window sill; these places just happen to be the most commonly suggested location because they typically get the most light. A desk, bookcase, or even a hanging pot is all perfectly reasonable locations too, so long as they get light. However, the real answer of where to grow it is anywhere. If you are using electric grow lamps to provide the required light your succulents need, then you could even grow them in a closet if you are providing the necessary light.

When it comes to picking a location for your succulents, start by looking at your window sills and seeing if they receive enough light to support a succulent naturally. If so, then this will be your best and cheapest choice. If yours don't provide enough light, you will need an electric grow light, which would allow you to grow your succulents anywhere. Start with your window sills, then work outwards from there.

Planting Succulent Seeds

Now that you know what size and make your containers are going to be, have mixed up the soil to fill them, and have even decided where in your house you'll grow your succulents, it is time to get actually *plant* your succulents. While many people will purchase their succulents already grown, many gardeners enjoy the prideful feeling that comes with taking a tiny seed and growing it into a beautiful plant. The feeling of going from seed to succulent is wonderful, and we'll be looking at how it is done so you too can experience the joy of it.

Growing a succulent isn't difficult and, as mentioned, they are quite easy to manage. However, growing a succulent from a seed will take more work. You need to be especially mindful of the conditions of your seeds through the germination and seedling stages of growth, which means a little more of your time and energy is going to be spent compared to purchasing already grown succulents, but don't let this turn you away. The wave of accomplishment you'll feel when your succulents first start to show their true colors will make it worth every second.

To begin, you will want to gather all the supplies you need. Always get everything you might need first, so you don't end up halfway through the planting process and realize that you need to run out to your local garden center. Get some shallow trays to plant the seeds in. These trays shouldn't be any deeper than four inches, and they should absolutely have drainage holes in the bottom. Next, you'll want some sand and some potting soil, both of which you should have around if you made your own soil. Purchase some plastic wrap to put over your seeds after they have been planted, a box of toothpicks to serve as a tiny shovel, and, of course, the seeds necessary to grow your chosen succulents.

You probably know what kind of succulent you want to grow. Chances are your reason for wanting to grow that kind is either due to how pretty it looks when it is fully grown, or for its medical or nutritious value, like an aloe would have. Regardless of what type, you should always research more about that species' growing times. Look up how long the germination process is for seeds like that and what type of climate they will want. You should also be mindful of where you buy the seeds. It is always best to go with a reputable commercial seller, as it is in their best interest to only sell the highest quality seeds and ensure that they provide the client with the right type of seeds. You'd be surprised how many people end up growing a different kind of succulent than they intended because the seeds they purchased didn't have any quality insurance before sale.

Whenever possible, use new trays for planting your seeds; however, this may not always be an option. If you have to reuse old trays, make sure that you wash them properly beforehand and let them dry out. You are going to fill up the trays with the potting mixture you made previously or by combining a mixture of coarse sand with potting soil. This soil should fill each tray you are using for seeds, so there is only about a half an inch of space between the top of the soil and the top of the tray. Regardless of which potting mixture you are going with, it is a good idea to pasteurize your soil prior to planting. This is done by baking the soil in an oven for half an hour at about 300°F. Take it out of the oven, allow it to cool down, then wet it with some clean water. Wait for the soil to completely drain before you pack it into the growing trays. This process is used to kill off any insects or harmful bacteria that might be swimming around in your soil. While older succulents are more resilient to these kinds of pests, young plants are much more

SUCCULENT GARDENING

susceptible to them and disease is far more likely to kill off young plants before they get a chance to flourish.

When it comes to growing plants, you will quickly notice that everything (except for the rare plant such as a peach tree) has small seeds. The largest plants grow from seeds so small you would think the end results impossible. Yet, when it comes to growing succulents, their seeds are even smaller than most. Succulents aren't very large plants, but the ratio from seed to plant is mind boggling—they're just so small. This can be a real pain because it makes it easy for them to run away on you. All it takes is a little breeze and your seeds could be scattered, forever lost. For this reason, it is best to deal with your seeds indoors and away from open windows or blowing fans.

SUCCULENT GARDENING

The first step to planting the seeds is to dampen the top layer of soil in each of the growing trays you plan to use. This is done to make each container a little more sticky, so the seeds hang onto the soil better. How many seeds you use in each individual container is going to depend on the needs of that kind of seedling. As we're primarily focused on using these small containers for seedlings only, spread out about four groupings of seeds per container. Later, as they grow, we will be transplanting the healthiest seedlings to their permanent homes and disposing of the weaker ones. Spread your seeds out across the soil, aiming to keep them an even distance apart from each other, with each seed taking up its own quarter.

Take a toothpick out of the box and use it to help you position your seeds. You could technically do this with your hands, but it is much more likely that the seeds will stick to your fingers when you do this. It is highly unlikely that they'll stick to a wooden toothpick, though. You'll want to have one or two seeds in each corner. So, if you divide the tray into quarters, you would have four different sections each with one or two seeds. This is done in case one of the seeds in a section doesn't germinate, so there would still be another one that will grow. Many plants will want you to dig a little hole to drop the seeds in, then cover them with soil. Succulents, on the other hand, just need to be kept on top of the soil.

SUCCULENT GARDENING

If you are planting more than one species, make sure you use a new growing tray for each. *Never* mix species together because they will then go on to fight each other over resources in the soil, and each of their needs will be slightly different. They will also have different growing rates, so when one is ready for transplant the other might not even be sprouting yet. You wouldn't toss a cat into a carrier along with a dog, so don't go growing an aloe in the same tray as a sunburst.

Once you have seeds in all of your containers, it is time to bust out the plastic wrap. Cover the tops of the containers with the plastic wrap, but make sure you don't obstruct the drainage holes on the bottom of the containers. This will help to keep harmful bacteria out of the containers and also keep the temperature and humidity at a better level for germination to happen. You will want to store these containers in a bright area but you should avoid storing them in direct sunlight, as this is much more likely to overheat them or burn the seedlings as they start to pop up. The temperature should be kept at roughly 70°F, though this is a generalization and you will want to check the requirements of each species you are growing first. The soil should be moist but never wet. Rot is a threat for succulents in general, but at this stage, it is even more likely that too much water will drown them. It tends to be better to mist the soil rather than water it. You should peel back the plastic wrap twice a day, misting it during one of these two times. The goal here is to allow air flow into the container for a few minutes. You can shorten this to once a day by poking some holes into the plastic wrap, though you shouldn't use anything bigger than a toothpick, as the plastic wrap will help protect the seeds from pests.

How long it takes for your seeds to germinate will vary based on the species. Some seeds only take a couple days to start sprouting into seedlings, whereas other types of succulents may take several weeks to do the same. There are even species that can take several months or even a year before they start. How long you have to wait will be determined by the species you are growing. It is probably a safe bet to assume that, as a new succulent grower, you have planted something in the days to weeks range. Remember to check your trays twice a day, once for airflow and once for both airflow and misting. Eventually, you will notice they have started to sprout up with tiny leaves forming. When you notice this occurrence, it is time to remove the plastic wrap. Some growers prefer to remove the plastic wrap during the day and put it back on at night. This isn't necessary, but it can help speed up the growing process a little bit. Whether you take it off completely or only during the day is up to you; just make sure you take it off completely before your succulent seedlings start pressing against it.

During the first couple weeks that your seedlings are visible, it is important to keep the soil nice and moist.

Watch that it is draining properly, as you don't want the plants drowning. At this stage in your succulents' lives, their root systems are growing and developing underneath the soil, and these roots need to be kept hydrated if they are to grow properly. As the roots become stronger, it becomes less important to keep the top layer of the soil moist. It should only take a couple weeks for this to happen, at which point you'll be wanting to move from daily misting to watering them once every week, in the same way that you will be watering them throughout their adult lives.

During these first couple weeks without the plastic wrap, you will want to start giving your seedlings more sunlight as you start to wean them off their misting schedule. The leaves of your seedlings will be maturing quite quickly at this point, and you will want to increase the amount of sunlight they receive while the leaves increase in size. You can expect to give them an extra hour of light once every three or four days. Do this until they are getting as much sunlight as they would on a typical day in the spot you have set out. This means that if the window sill you decided on gets twelve hours of sunlight in a day, you will slowly increase how much sunlight your seedlings get, an extra hour at a time, until they are used to getting twelve hours.

Finally, the tray that you planted your succulent seeds in shouldn't be the same tray that you expect them to live in their entire lives. It will take a few months before they are big enough to be transplanted and, with succulents, it is better to wait a little longer than to do it too early. You should expect to keep them in their first trays for six months or so after first sprouting. To transplant, you will need to loosen up the soil they are growing in, take the plant by the base of the stem, then gently lift it out. The root ball should be nice and tight, which will make it much easier to do this. Use your fingers to brush off any soil that is sticking to the plant and pull off any dead roots that are sticking out. Set up your new container as discussed in the soil section of this chapter, but only to the halfway mark. You will want to put the root ball in, secure the plant, then fill up the rest of the soil. It is a good idea to use your fingers to gently pack in the soil around the base, so it is firmly kept in place. Most plants want to be watered immediately after transplanting, but not succulents. It is better to wait a couple days before watering them, as they will need time to get settled into their new homes.

There you have it. You have now grown a succulent from seed to adulthood. It's a simple process, though it requires you to pay attention to and mist the soil they are growing in. Another way to grow succulents is to take clippings and plant them, though this first requires a full grown succulent. For the time being, try your hand at growing from seed, so you get experience with each stage of the succulent's growth cycle.

SUCCULENT GARDENING

Fertilizer for Succulents

Succulents need nutrients if they are to stay healthy and continue to grow. In this way, they're no different from any other plant that you may choose to grow. Succulents grown indoors will need to be fertilized less often than those grown outdoors, but they still benefit from having a fertilizing schedule setup. Remember to keep in mind that indoor succulents need less fertilizer than other indoor plants, as too much fertilizer will increase the chances of rot. This is especially true of fertilizers that are high in nitrogen, as succulents have a particularly rough time dealing with too much nitrogen.

The best bet for succulents is to use a fertilizer that has been NPK balanced at either 8-8-8 or 10-10-10. This means that it has an even ratio of nitrogen (N), phosphorus (P) and potassium (K). You can purchase sprays already mixed to this ratio, though it is cheaper to purchase a water soluble mixture that you would dissolve into a gallon of water. Succulents don't need as much fertilizer as other plants, so it is a good idea to make your fertilizer mixture half as strong as is recommended on the package. If you are growing succulents that hail from tropical climates, then these should be watered more often and fed a fertilizer mix that is only a quarter of the recommended dosage.

Slowly feed your fertilizer mixture to your succulents. As you feed, you will start to notice liquid draining from the drainage holes at the bottom of the container. When you notice this, it is time to move onto feeding the next succulent. Fertilizer should only be used on succulents during the spring and the summer, and no later than early in the fall. During the dormant season in the winter, you will want to avoid fertilizing succulents, as this will only confuse them. Fertilizer should only be fed to your succulents as long as the top inch of the soil is completely dry. It is better to put off a fertilizing session for a week to let the soil dry rather than fertilize moist soil, as this will only promote the conditions necessary for your succulents to start rotting.

SUCCULENT GARDENING

Chapter Summary

- It is a rule of thumb that the more green a succulent is, the better suited it will be to an indoor garden.

- There are many species that do well indoors, such as jade plants, flaming katys, snake plants, and roseums.

- Growing succulents indoors doesn't take as much time and attention as many other indoor crops would, but they still demand the proper conditions if they are to stay healthy.

- To grow succulents indoors, you will need containers, shears, a spade, a way of reading the pH level of the soil, a liquid fertilizer, potting soil, toothpicks, and seeds. You will also want a fan for good airflow if you don't already have one, though this can be worked around if necessary.

- Picking the best container to grow your succulents in requires a consideration of size, material and drainage. Each of these pieces need to be looked at and weighed against each other to decide the best container for your succulents.

- Terracotta is a porous material, which is good because it makes it easier for your succulents to dry off. However, during hot seasons, terracotta holds onto a lot of heat, which can cause your succulents to burn.

SUCCULENT GARDENING

- Plastic is a cheaper material, and its lightweight design makes it a favorite of general growers. Plastic doesn't breathe well, so it will need lots of drainage in the form of drainage holes at the bottom and a loose potting soil mixture.

- Ceramic containers come in glazed and unglazed varieties. Unglazed is a lot like terracotta, though it doesn't breathe quite as well. Glazed ceramic doesn't breathe at all, and it is likely a poor choice for beginning gardeners.

- Glass, concrete, resin, and wood are all options for containers, but these four materials will likely not be a great fit for your succulents.

- Your best bet is going with plastic, terracotta, or unglazed ceramic. Keep in mind that the schedule you water your succulents will, in part, depend entirely on how quickly the soil in their containers dries up, and material plays a large part in this.

- The size of a container should be matched to the needs of the plant and, with succulents, this means the size of the plant's roots. The bigger the root system, the bigger the container. Succulents tend to have shorter root systems, so they grow best in a smaller container.

- A deeper container can be harmful to a succulent because water has to travel through more soil to escape, and the roots of your succulent don't get to enjoy that extra water because it has reached so deep. Therefore, it is all risk with no reward.

- Containers made out of glass are unlikely to have drainage holes, but most containers you look at should have some in the bottom. It is recommended that you only use pots with drainage holes. To use a container without a drainage hole will greatly increase the difficulty of tending for your succulents.

- If you are going to purchase a pre-made potting soil, make sure it is a quick draining soil with lots of minerals in it.

- To make your own succulent soil for your indoor plants, you will need to mix together three ingredients. By controlling how much of each you add, you can change the texture of the potting soil at will. If it is your first time making a potting soil mixture, stick with even parts for each ingredient.

- The first ingredient is an all purpose potting soil. Get one that doesn't have any vermiculite added in as it will only serve to retain moisture. Mix in coarse sand like that used for a backyard sandbox instead, which will improve drainage. Also add in perlite, which will further increase the drainage of your soil. Stir these all together in equal parts.

SUCCULENT GARDENING

- Fill up the containers you are planning to grow in. Any extra indoor succulent soil can be stored in an air proof container for further use down the road.

- You can grow your succulents anywhere you like inside, but the best places will be near windows where they can receive enough sunlight to keep growing. Direct sunlight isn't the best, so consider how you can provide partial cover throughout the day.

- Indoor succulents can be grown with electronic lights if necessary, which can help you control the growing environment more carefully.

- Succulents need a minimum of six hours of sun. If a succulent isn't receiving enough light, you may notice it starting to grow tall and thin. This is because it is trying to grow in such a way that it can reach the sun. Prevent this by carefully selecting your locations.

- You will want to rotate your succulents a couple times a week, as they will bend toward the sun when they grow naturally. Turning the succulent every couple of days will change the direction of the bend and help keep your plants growing straight.

- It isn't hard to grow a succulent. Most growers use the clippings from adult plants to propagate new plants; however, growing from seed is still a time tested favorite way for new gardeners to get started.

- Get your containers together, some plastic wrap, seeds, and toothpicks to care for your succulents.

- Succulent seeds are super tiny, so you'll want to be careful when working with them. Different seeds have different germination and growing times, so only plant one kind of succulent in each container. That said, you can fit a couple succulents into a container together while they're young like this.

- If you are worried about harmful bacteria getting in your garden, you can bake your potting soil before using it.

- Use a spray bottle to dampen the top layer of soil in your growing trays, so the tiny seeds don't go spilling all over the place. Seeds don't need to be buried, so wetting the soil a little will help keep them where you want them. Since they are likely to stick to your fingers, use your toothpick to move them around as necessary.

- Cover your newly seeded containers in plastic wrap. Twice a day, you will peel back the plastic wrap. The first time will be to mist the top of the soil, while the second is simply to allow better airflow to your seeds.

SUCCULENT GARDENING

- Once your seedlings are visible, you will need to remove the plastic wrap. You will slowly stop misting the soil over a period of a couple weeks until they are only being watered once a week.

- After you remove the plastic wrap, you will start to introduce your succulents to more sunlight. Every few days, start giving them an hour more of sunlight until they are eventually receiving their full amount every day.

- Replant your succulents by being mindful of the root ball and giving them a few days to get used to their new home before watering them again. It will likely take around six months before your seedlings are big enough to replant.

- Succulents need a fertilizer mix that is NPK balanced. Avoid any fertilizers that are high in nitrogen. Succulents don't need much fertilizer, so don't use an overly strong batch. Slowly feed your succulents the mixture until you notice the liquid draining from the holes of the container. Only fertilize your succulents in the spring until the early fall (reverse this for winter succulents).

- Only fertilize your succulents when the top inch of the soil is dry.

SUCCULENT GARDENING

In the next chapter, you will learn all about growing succulents outdoors. From picking a location with enough sun or shade to properly preparing the soil and fertilizing the plants, the next chapter has everything you need to know about traditionally grown succulents.

CHAPTER FOUR

HOW TO GROW SUCCULENTS OUTDOORS

If succulents make for a beautiful addition to any household, then they will make a gorgeous addition to your landscaping efforts. Succulents can be used in so many neat and interesting ways to really bring your yard or your outdoor garden to life. When grown outdoors, succulents can be planted directly in the ground, or they can be grown in containers used to augment your already-existing garden. To grow succulents in a container outdoors has much more in common with growing succulents indoors when compared to those succulents grown in the ground. In this chapter, we will focus on those grown in the ground, but you should keep in mind that combining the information about growing outdoors with the information about growing succulents in a container from the last chapter will provide you everything you need to know to work with outdoor succulents in containers, if you so desire.

In this chapter, we will first consider the best locations to grow an outdoor succulent. This section will combine practical requirements with aesthetic options, and you might just be surprised at how many options succulents give to us gardeners. You'll want to choose an outdoor variety like sedum, sempervivum, kalanchoe, or aeonium, but even in this small selection listed, there is a wide range of styles and looks. Once you have a location chosen, you will need to consider the soil that you use. While you could just rely on the soil already in the ground, it is better to play an active role in shaping the soil through the addition of sand and other materials. Primarily, our goal with shaping the soil is to create a fast-draining mixture to keep our succulents healthy. Finally, we'll look at another way to make a fertilizer that our succulents just love and we'll see how feeding plants differs when they are outdoors.

Picking the Best Location for Outdoor Succulents

When it comes to picking the best location, there are quite a few more considerations that we must take for outdoor succulents when compared to those that we raise inside. Since we don't have the same level of control over the outdoors than we do when we are inside, we need to really pay attention to the weather (storms, freezes, swinging temperatures, and more will all have the potential to damage our succulents), the sun (too much and our plants will burn), the drainage and dampness of the location (too much and our succulents will rot), the amount of space they have (their interactions with other plants could be harmful), the quality of the soil (which we'll learn more about in a few moments), and even how they look in any given space. Each of these issues can make or break your outdoor succulents, so it is important to take each of them into consideration when picking the perfect location to grow your plants. Considering each of them in depth now will make it crystal clear just how important they all are.

When it comes to the weather, our succulents each will have their own needs and desires. In general, succulents want warm weather. They prefer to have a temperature that stays within a set range; anything too high and they will burn up, and anything too low will present its own difficulties (we'll look at how succulents handle winter in chapter six). Being a few degrees above or below their prefered temperature isn't going to kill them. What will hurt them, however, is *swings* in the temperature. If you live in an area that sees a large variation in the temperature over a short period of time then this will greatly confuse your succulents and it could even throw their entire schedule off. Almost nothing is worse than having plants going dormant when they are supposed to be blooming.

SUCCULENT GARDENING

Temperature aside, succulents are quite resilient little plants, but this doesn't mean they are invincible. Powerful storms can rip succulents out of the ground and send them flying. If the roots hold, then the leaves or flowers can be battered to the point of dismemberment or the need to amputate. This later experience is even worse for your plants, as they are shocked when the damage first happens, then take a second shock while you work to repair it by moving the damaged leaves or stems. If storms or fluctuations in temperature are a large concern in your area, then you might be best off planting your succulents in containers that you can bring inside during unhealthy weather. Many gardeners prefer the flexibility to move their outdoor succulents inside at times like these, and some gardeners like taking their indoor succulents outside during the summer. If you want to plant your succulents directly into the ground, then consider how your chosen location is protected from strong winds. Growing succulents alongside fences, houses, or larger plants that can act as protection will increase their longevity.

As mentioned multiple times throughout this book, succulents actually don't want a whole lot of direct sunlight. Chances are good that this will be mentioned again before the end of the book, as it is one of the biggest and most popular misconceptions out there when it comes to growing succulents. People think of cacti and deserts and assume that succulents just *adore* the sun. There are exceptions to every rule, so while some succulents love the sun, most of them have a more impartial relationship to it—they love to be around the sun, but only on their own terms. If you think that a sunburnt succulent is some kind of joke, then go ahead and plant yours in full sunlight. I can promise that watching the leaves of your beautiful new succulent start to brown and burn is enough to break any gardener's heart.

If you want to keep your succulents nice and healthy with just the right amount of sunlight, then you will want to plant them in the shade. The best shade to choose is partial shade, which means you are going to want to pay attention to how a particular location is shaded (or not) throughout the day. As you narrow down the locations in your garden that you want to grow some succulents, set up a schedule to check on how its shade changes throughout the day. If you can't check on this in person, you could set up a camera to take a photo every thirty minutes while you are away. What this will do is let you see exactly how long a particular area receives direct sunlight and how long it gets shade. The perfect area is a combination of the two. Succulents will want to get about six hours of sunlight and some species will want even more. Flowering plants tend to need a minimum of eight, for example. By tracking how the sun and shade affect the area you are going to grow your succulents, you will know exactly how much sunlight your plants are getting to ensure they grow properly.

It is a good idea to use a thermometer to check the temperature of the spot, both when it is in shade and when it is in direct sunlight. There are a lot of succulents that will see their color fade or develop unseemly spots when in temperatures above 90°F. This isn't a result of burning, but rather another risk added alongside it that shows just how much succulents don't actually enjoy direct sunlight. It is important to get these readings prior to planting, as even a partially shaded location can get too hot during the hours when the sun is the highest, typically from noon until the evening. During these hours, the addition of a shade cloth may be necessary to bring the temperature down to safe levels.

The next concern is the drainage of your chosen location. Note that the order of concerns does not denote a hierarchy of importance. Except for the aesthetic appeal, each of these concerns about location should be considered equally, as a location that fails to pass any one concern will need to be altered in some way to overcome this lack. If you choose an area with too much direct sunlight, then you will need to add shade. If you choose an area in which the elements are going to damage your succulents, then you need to add protection. If you choose an area with poor drainage, you will need to fix it. Note, this isn't even referring to the soil itself—we'll be talking about the soil in a moment, but first, there are other concerns about drainage that have to be considered.

Is your yard on a slope? If so, water will naturally move downward over your lawn. Is your yard uneven? Then there will be natural pockets that can capture lots of water when it rains or when the snow melts. In these two examples, the lower part of your yard and the pockets just mentioned are going to soak up much more water than the rest of the yard. It's a smart idea to plant really thirsty plants in these areas, but it is a terrible idea to plant succulents here. Too much sun? Succulents burn. Too much water? They rot. When it comes to picking the right location, you are trying to seek the perfect balance between the two. Succulents planted in the areas from the example would be high risk plants.

SUCCULENT GARDENING

Considering your yard by way of drainage would reveal a few generalizations that can make picking a space easier. It is better to have succulents planted on the tops of hills than at the bottom—in your yard, this doesn't need to be a very high hill whatsoever. Elevating your succulents through raised beds or mounds will not only provide much greater drainage, but it will also add texture to your yard and can make for some of the most beautiful gardens through the 3D quality that it gives a property. We'll look briefly at how to build a succulent rock garden before the end of the chapter. Another generalization is that tighter ground will equal worse drainage. We'll get more into this when we get to preparing the soil for our outdoor succulents, but first, there's still more we need to consider about location.

Succulents should be given their own space when planted outdoors. These plants are a beautiful, small size that makes them a great fit for lining pathways or outlining the edges of a garden bed. However, when being grown around other plants, they should be given enough space to do their own thing or be planted in containers which can then be buried under the dirt to keep them aligned properly. Succulents grow slower than other plants, which means that it can be hard for new gardeners to judge exactly how much space is needed for each succulent, and between succulents and other plants. The space itself, when planted too close to other types of plants such as flowers or vegetables then the difference in watering and fertilizing, needs to be taken into account when treating that garden bed.

All that said, succulents need to be spaced fairly close together to promote upward growth rather than outward growth. That is, if you plant a succulent alone, it is going to grow to be a wider plant because of all the space it has. When grown with other succulents, if they are spaced the right distance apart, then they will grow upwards instead. This control will allow you to really play around with the look of the succulents in your garden, though it requires a careful consideration of the space you have to grow them. Different species have different needs regarding space, so research is just as important here as it is with temperature or watering needs.

As mentioned, the quality of the soil is an important consideration of space; however, this is something that we can take more control of by mixing our own soil. We will be doing this in a minute, but for now, take note that, if we can't take control of the soil in one location, then we should forget about that area and focus on looking for a location in which we can control the soil.

The whole point of growing succulents in your garden in the first place is almost always because they're beautiful plants. The color, size, and shape are all important factors in why they are chosen in the first place. Succulents are really beautiful, and when well-managed they can fit into so many awesome designs.

SUCCULENT GARDENING

While considering if the spaces you've been checking out match the needs of your plants, you should also consider how many great options they give you in terms of looks. The following section will outline some of the coolest ways to add succulents to your outdoor garden.

Succulents can be used to make a mosaic. Select three or four different succulents based on their shape and color, and grow them together in different designs and patterns. So long as the plants require the same general climate, you can make beautiful, captivating mosaics. Some people like to use succulents to create a groundcover to help keep maintenance costs of their yards down. Since succulents are able to weather through droughts, it helps to keep moisture in the area in a way that would benefit the soil. Others like to line pathways or garden boxes with succulents. Their bright colors contrast really well against lighter rocks, so one of the most popular homes for succulents are rock gardens. You'll learn how to make your own rock garden before the end of the chapter. Another really cool way to plant some succulents is to take an old barrel, turn it on its side and pack it full of soil or half bury it in your garden. Plant succulents inside to create a country style home for your plants.

Speaking of soil, we will be looking at how outdoor plants can be helped out with the right succulent soil in the next section.

Succulent Soil for Outdoor Plants

The soil requirements for succulents that are grown outdoors aren't as restrictive as those grown in containers. As the argument for growing succulents outdoors says, plants are naturally grown outdoors after all. However, this doesn't mean that you should just toss your plant into the dirt and hope for the best. It is better to take into consideration their soil needs as potted, then adjust based on environmental sustainability.

The best soil for succulents is always going to be one that drains quickly. Too much moisture, your succulents rot. Even outdoors, we want soil that drains quickly. Succulents do the best in soil that has lots of sand or gravel in it, which is why they are so fitting for rock gardens. Succulents are used to soil that gets soaked but then quickly dries out, so any soil we make needs this factor. When growing in a container we have drainage holes at the bottom to help moisture escape but this isn't an option to us when we are growing in the ground itself. Plants grown outdoors in the ground have to rely on the sun to help them dry off. The combination of sunlight and fresh air will dry out your succulents and their soil by evaporating the water. Soils with lots of drainage make it easier for water to escape through this process. Rather than seeping out the bottom of a container, the water actually escapes back the way it came.

Since succulents are used to rocky soil, the best way to understand what ratio your soil should be is to consider the difference between organic and mineral pieces. Something organic is something that is or was at one point alive. Minerals are naturally forming elements that have never been alive. Compost, leaves, bark, trigs—all of these are organic substances used in the soil. Rocks and sand are minerals. The organic elements in soil provide nutrients and are able to soak up water. The minerals on the other hand don't soak up water, so this helps to promote drainage and reduce the levels of moisture in the ground. Succulents really enjoy having a lot of minerals where they grow and, while some gardeners use a formula with a ratio 60% organic and 40% mineral, there are others who use a ratio of 20% organic and 80% mineral. The main idea is that the more minerals in your mixture, the better.

While we mixed together potting soil for our indoor plants in the last chapter, we're going to mix together our own here as well. We'll be following a slightly different recipe this time. This recipe can also be used for indoor plants—consider it another way of making soil for your succulents that you can choose from. Alternatively, if you came right to this chapter, then you won't need to worry about flipping back to the other for a perfectly effective succulent soil.

SUCCULENT GARDENING

This simple recipe aims for a 33% organic to 66% mineral mixture, which is achieved by mixing together one third organic with two thirds mineral. The organic component will always be one third of the same, but you can (and should) combine two different minerals together for the best results. Simply take an organic mixture of either potting soil, pine bark, compost, or coconut coir, and measure out how much you use. This amount then becomes one third. Use a mineral-like coarse sand, gravel, volcanic rock, or perlite, and measure out an equal amount to the organic substance you picked. Measure this same amount again with a different mineral, then mix it all up together, either using a tool or your hands (so long as you've washed and dried them already). That's all it takes to make your own soil, but there are a few pointers to consider when picking the ingredients.

SUCCULENT GARDENING

When selecting a potting soil, it is best to avoid those with peat. When peat dries out, it starts to repel and push water away. It's what is called **hydrophobic**. What this means when it comes to watering, peat needs to be slowly soaked and careful tended to. Peat takes a lot of watering and really needs to soak liquid in deep, which isn't good for succulents that start to rot when moisture is trapped. Sand is a great addition to any soil, but it needs to be coarse sand; otherwise, it won't do the trick, and beach sand should be avoided as it can hurt you succulents. Perlite looks a bit like vermiculite, but the latter holds onto moisture in a really mean way. Gravel should be cleaned to remove any infectious particles it might have on it, and it should be mixed into the soil rather than used as a layer on the bottom or top of the mixture.

You now have a wonderful soil mixture that a succulent will love, regardless of if it is indoors or outdoors. So, what changes when brought outside? Succulents are less particular than those grown in containers, and they can deal with a little more variety in their soil; however, they still want a gritty mixture, so this soil is perfect for them. Their soil doesn't need to drain quite as well as the soil indoor succulents use, thanks to evaporation, but they still benefit from quick draining soil, so your new soil mixture will still be effective.

If you have gone with a mixture that avoided peat moss, then your new soil will be a sustainable soil that will help keep the ground healthy. This ultimately means that by mixing together your own soil, you will also be assisting your yard itself. Not only will this leave your succulents growing beautifully, but it will also help keep everything growing longer.

Of course, one option for growing your succulents is to focus on rocks instead of dirt. It's time to see how this is achieved.

Succulents on the Rocks: Building Your Own Succulent Rock Garden

Many succulents prefer to live with rocks than with flowers down in the soil. Rock gardens are especially great places to plant succulents because their colors pop against the mineral colors, and they can manage their water and moisture needs more easily in these environments. The first step in designing a succulent rock garden is to pick a type of succulent that grows well on rocks. The following list of succulents contains just a few examples:

- Angelina (*sedum reflexum*)

- Irene (*sempervivum heuffelii*)

- Little Missy (*sedum*)

- Henri Correvon (*sempervivum heuffelii*)

SUCCULENT GARDENING

- Parodia erubescens

- Sedum album

- Lime gold (*sedum adolphii*)

- Orange ice (*sedum album*)

- Blue jelly bean (*sedum pachyphyllum*)

- Mystique (*sempervivum heuffelii*)

- Neon breakers (*echeveria*)

- Crassula rubricaulis

- Gold moss (*sedum acre*)

- Ogon (*sedum makinoi*)

- Starshine (*sempervivum*)

- Mona Lisa (*sempervivum*)

- Silk pinwheel (*aeonium arboreum*)

- Black pearl (*sedum album*)

- Turquoise tails (*sedum sediforme*)

SUCCULENT GARDENING

While this is far from all the succulents you could possibly have in your rock garden, it provides many possible combinations of beautiful patterns, and both in shape and color. These plants can be the main attraction in a rock garden or be used to fill in the space between rocks with bright, beautiful colors. Using the knowledge you've gained on picking a location, you're going to pick a spot that receives plenty of sun in the morning but shade from afternoon to sundown. Once you do, it's time to start scaping the land a little.

Take your soil mixture from the previous step and mix up a lot of it. Use the soil and rocks and start creating peaks and valleys, building up little mounds, or even one large mound. The elevation of this and the fact that it is done with a succulent soil will give it plenty of drainage to prevent succulent rot. Be careful to ensure that your alterations don't ruin the shade they are receiving throughout the afternoon. Use boulders and large rocks to help shape the space. A simple and popular design is to create a circle with the rocks tightly packed together to hold up the soil where the succulents will be planted. Rocks can be mixed in and around as much as desired.

Plant your succulents and let them start to fill out and bring beautiful colors to your rock garden. If you live in an area with occasional rain, you won't even need to water your rock garden. Nine times out of ten, a rock garden will do just fine on rain alone. However, this isn't an excuse to ignore the plants—checking up on them throughout the growing process is a must, even when they're practically raising themselves.

SUCCULENT GARDENING

Growing Succulents from Seeds

Growing succulents from seeds should be done in containers indoors before they are taken out and replanted in the garden. This process was covered in depth in the last chapter but a quick run of the steps will serve as a crash course for those that came straight to outdoor growing.

Succulents should be planted in short trays with drainage holes along the bottom. Your outdoor soil mixture is a perfect mix for seeds to be grown in, so just fill the containers up to an inch away from the top. The top of the soil should be damp, so the seeds stick, as succulent seeds are amazingly small. Spread the seeds out on the top of the soil and don't cover them with any more soil. Only use a few seeds per container, the exact number you should use depends on the size of the succulents you are planting, so err on the side of caution. Different types should be grown in different containers to begin with.

After the seeds are in the container, cover the top with plastic lid and store it in an area with lots of light, but no direct sunlight, as such is too strong for weaker plants. Keep them around a temperature of 70°F and check them twice a day, peeling back the plastic wrap once to mist the soil with water and a second time to promote airflow. It could take some days or weeks for these new plants to start growing. Once you see leaves start to come out, it is time to remove the plastic lid during the day. Continue misting the soil for the first couple weeks, and slowly back off to start watering them weekly instead. Start introducing them to sunlight, an hour at a time up to their adult normal. If they are plants that want six hours, they would first start with an hour a day, then after a couple days, bump it up to two hours a day. This would follow until they are receiving six hours a day like they are going to when planted outdoors.

The most important difference when it comes to growing seeds for outdoor gardens comes with the replanting of those succulents when they are ready to leave the containers. Indoor gardeners will replant them into new containers, but outdoor gardeners will plant them back into the ground. One of the biggest shocks that a new plant can undergo is a massive change in its environment. In this respect, what is meant by the environment is the growing media that it has been living in. If you are using the same soil mixture you use for your outdoor succulents, then this won't be a problem at all. If you are planning on using a different soil, then this will be a riskier activity, and you will need to pay closer attention to the newly moved plants.

It will typically take six months or more before a succulent is ready to be replanted. Once it is, you will shake free the soil around the root ball, so it is easy to remove. Succulents have tight root balls, which helps to make it an easier process. As long as you've washed and dried your hands, you can use them to brush away soil and any dead plant matter that the seedling is hanging onto. Dig a small hole and put the root ball inside. Cover it back up with soil until it roughly covered the same as it had been, then you can pack the soil in tightly around the base of the succulent to keep it in place.

Even though the new plant is in the same kind of soil as it had been before, it is going to take a little bit of time for it to adjust. If you've ever had a cat, you've probably seen how, even though they've seen a house before, it takes them time to adjust to a new one. Plants are just as fussy, so give it some time before you water it again. If you would normally water it once a week, try moving it in the middle of the cycle, so it has half a week to get used to the new soil before it is watered again on schedule. This will help it have an easier time settling into its new home outdoors.

Fertilizing Your Outdoor Succulents

While succulents aren't the most demanding of plants, they still benefit from receiving fertilizer to help them grow big and bright. The right nutrients mixed into a liquid form will provide your succulents with the tender and loving care they need to absolutely flourish. Of course, too much or too strong of a fertilizer, and your succulents will feel the pain of nutrient burn the same way any other plant would. You can't overfeed your plants, so it is important to be careful when using your fertilizer and monitor the reactions you are seeing from your succulents.

There are several brands of fertilizer tea available on the market. This kind of fertilizer is easy to use and will treat your succulents well without burning them out. This is a different approach to fertilizer than was used to treat our indoor succulents but this doesn't necessarily make it any better or any worse. Both methods are perfectly valid, so if you already mixed up a batch of fertilizer, then you'll be good to go already and can skip ahead to application. For the rest of us, it's time to make tea.

Fertilizer tea, otherwise known as *manure tea*, is an organic solution to fertilizer needs. Both compost and manure are great additions to most garden soil, as it provides plenty of nutrients for the soil and the plants therein. However, it is quite a messy approach (that you should definitely wear gloves for). It also smells horrible. Fertilizer tea, on the other hand, is a cleaner and less smelly way to provide your succulents with a great boost. There are many brands, such as Haven Brand Manure Tea, that you can choose from, either online or through your local garden center. When you open up the package, you will find what looks like a large but otherwise normal tea bag. This is going to be the source of your fertilizer, so don't go accidentally grabbing it instead of the Earl Gray.

Get yourself a bucket or a container that is at least a gallon. The perfect size would be five gallons, as you can make a ton of this stuff at one time. Fill up your container with water, but make sure that you pour it over the bag. The water may be room temperature or cold, but otherwise, treat it like you were pouring the world's largest tea. You'll want the water to be pretty much on the top. Tie the tea bag to the container, so it will rest inside and float by the top of the water. The larger the container you brew it in, the weaker the fertilizer will be. However, it is better to have a weaker fertilizer than a stronger one when you are starting out. If you can only mix together a single gallon, then be mindful to cut it with more water before giving it to your succulents. But first, it needs to be brewed.

Place a cover over top of your container and place it out of the way somewhere for a few days. When you first put the bucket away, the water will be a sickly yellow-ish color. After three or four days when you are ready to open it back up, you'll see that it is now a disgusting brown color. Toss on a pair of gloves and remove the tea bag, which should be easy since you tied it to the side. You can toss out the tea bag and start using this fertilizer. If you brewed it in a five gallon jug, then it will be a wonderful consistency for your succulents, and stronger teas should be watered down a bit. You can pour this into a spray bottle to apply it slowly over a longer period of time, or you can fill up a watering can with it and treat it like a normal watering session for your succulents. Since applying once and waiting for results is the easiest method, it is recommended for beginners.

You should notice a difference within a month. Succulents love fertilizer tea, and it induces a growing spurt. Within two months, your succulents should grow big and bright and really fill out the space that they are in. Since fertilizer tea is rather weak, you won't need to worry about damaging your succulents through overfeeding them. The weakness of it does allow you some more options when it comes to application. A spray bottle filled with manure tea could be used every other week if desired. If you prefer pouring at once, then this could be done once a month, but you might not see any more impressive growth than you would with fertilizing once a year. Remember that fertilizer should only be used around spring or fall, depending on whether their growing season is in the summer (feed in spring) or winter (feed in fall). Fertilizer tea allows plenty of flexibility for you to fine-tune and perfect your timing based on the needs of your plant. When in doubt, listen to them.

SUCCULENT GARDENING

Chapter Summary

- Picking the best location for your outdoor succulents requires a consideration of the space in your yard.

- Succulents do best when they receive direct sunlight for a small part of the day and lots of shade for the rest of the day. Picking a space that gets plenty of shade is important, but you can always create your own shade if you need to.

- Pay attention to the way that your property is sloped. Water naturally travels into the valleys created by your landscape, and this means they start moist for much longer than usual. Avoid planting succulents in spaces like this, as it just invites troubles like root rot and infestation.

- Pay attention to the temperature in areas you are considering, and see how it changes throughout the day. You don't want your succulents to be so hot that they burn.

- Succulents enjoy having their own space when planted outside. They have certain conditions around their placing, such as being placed close together to control whether they grow outwards or upwards.

SUCCULENT GARDENING

- The best soil for your outdoor succulents is very close to that used by your indoor succulents. It needs to drain quickly. We use a mixture of organic material, like soil or compost, and mineral material, like rocks and sand. Combining one part organic matter with two parts mineral matter will create a wonderful soil for your succulents.

- Succulents do really great in rock gardens, which can be made by selecting some rocks and using them to build up a vertical display. Rock gardens done in this way have great drainage and dry off quickly, making them perfect for succulents.

- Succulent seeds are tiny and can be easily lost. Thankfully, it is easy to grow by seed. Follow the steps in growing your seeds indoors, but then transplant them outside rather than into a larger container.

- One way to fertilize your outdoor succulents is to make a batch of fertilizer tea and feed it to them. Creating a mixture that doesn't spike the pH level of the soil is the best idea since you can give plenty of this kind of fertilizer to your succulents.

- You only need to fertilize once a year if you feed it all to your succulents at once, but some gardeners like to slowly feed fertilizer to their succulents throughout the growing season. Just make sure that you stop feeding them as they transition out of the growing season.

- If you feed your succulents all at once, you will notice a difference almost right away in how they start to take off. Within two months, you should see some amazing growth.

In the next chapter, you will learn what goes into tending your succulent plants. Between questions of when to and how much water to give them and the proper time to prune them, the following chapter makes caring for your succulents simple. You will also learn how to avoid common issues like disease, rot, and pests, so your plants stay healthy and beautiful.

CHAPTER FIVE

CARING FOR SUCCULENT PLANTS

Throughout the book, the care of your succulents has been an important point of discussion. From avoiding strong fertilizers that could cause nutrient burn to providing shade to prevent sunburn and promoting quick drainage to avoid succulent rot, health and care should be the top priority when it comes to your plants. After all, these are living organisms under your care. In this chapter, we'll see exactly what care needs to be taken after they are growing healthily in the ground or in a container.

Watering your succulents can be a dangerous exercise if you don't pay attention to your plants, so we'll cover both indoor and outdoor watering first. From watering, it is a small step to succulent rot, and we'll cover this annoying phenomenon in depth to see just exactly how it is. Pruning is a step in maintaining just about every type of plant known to man, but this exercise also shocks plants, so it must be done at the right times and with their safety in mind. Finally, even when all of that goes fine, your succulents might still end up being dinner to a colony of pests. Preventing pests from infesting your plants can be easy, but repelling them after they've gotten a foothold can be miserable.

When and How to Water Your Succulents

Too little watering and your succulents won't grow nearly as much as they should. Too much and you could kill them entirely. The hardest part about raising succulents is figuring out exactly when you are supposed to water them. However, just because it is the hardest part doesn't mean it has to be that hard. Just pay attention to your plants—follow the steps and use the feedback you get from your plants, along with your common sense to fine-tune your watering schedule and techniques.

If you have been following the advice throughout the book so far, then your indoor succulents will already be housed in containers with drainage holes. If they are not, then you are going to need to take extra care to make sure they aren't being overwatered. If you are a beginner to growing succulents, then you should avoid containers without drainage. You also need to make sure that the soil can drain well. If you mixed your own, then this should be no problem; however, if it doesn't drain well, then watering your plants is going to be a dangerous mindfield, and rot is sure to take hold at the first opportunity. Finally, you can use a spray bottle if you are applying a strong fertilizer, but when it comes to water, you will want to soak them when you water them. Seedlings get misted instead of soaked, but once succulents are adults, they need lots of water in the soil in long intervals.

Indoor succulents should be watered roughly once a week. The best way to water indoor succulents is to take inspiration from the **hydroponic ebb & flow method**. Completely and totally soak the soil in the container when you are watering your succulent. After this is complete, you must wait until the soil entirely dried out before you water again. It should equal out to one watering a week, give or take a couple days. If you have plastic containers, you can pick them up and check their weights to see if the soil has dried out. Containers made of other material can be checked with the finger method—insert a finger two inches or more into the soil to see if it is moist or dry. Don't water until it is fully dry.

Even if the soil is completely dry, you may want to wait a day or two extra before watering. Succulents are resistant to drought, so dry conditions aren't too dangerous to them. This can allow you to stay on the side of caution; by letting them dry a couple extra days, you encourage new root growth, which helps them stay strong and healthy. It can also help you propagate new plants by splitting the root ball in two and replanting both halves. So that covers indoor succulents, but what about those grown outdoors?

Outdoor succulents are going to be watered in much the same way that your indoor ones are. You don't control the temperature outside like you do indoors, which means that how long it takes the soil outside to dry depends on how hot it is. Often, this means that you will need to water your plants several times a week during the summer, but maybe only once a week during the fall. Plants grown in containers outside tend to need more watering than those grown in the ground. Outdoor succulents tend to be thirstier, but care is still important to avoid overwatering.

Identifying, Preventing and Treating Succulent Root Rot

Root rot can sneak up on you and kill off your succulents quicker than you can spot it if you don't know what you're looking for. Even the most careful of gardeners can let their standards slip and wake up to find dead plants. Prevention of root rot has been stressed throughout the book, so it's high time you learn exactly what this nuisance is.

As it turns out, it's a lot of things—**root rot** is a term used to refer to a whole bunch of diseases that attack the plant's roots. These diseases come in two varieties, but both types are terrible; the first variety just quickly kills your plant, while the second, although still killing your plant in the end, this time it does so slowly. Neither type is a lot of fun. The primary cause behind root rot is too much moisture in the soil, which prevents the roots of the succulent from breathing. As it has been stressed multiple times now, drowning your plant will cause the roots to start rotting. The best way to avoid root rot is to take steps to prevent it, so let's look at those first.

Root rot can be caused by disease or pathological factors like bacteria. You aren't likely to deal with the pathological kind, however. If you are worried about it, then you can toss your potting soil in the oven for half an hour. Bake it to kill off any harmful bacteria prior to planting. Overwatering becomes the biggest risk at that point—if you followed the steps we discussed above, then you shouldn't have to deal with root rot. Prevention comes in the form of using a quick draining soil and being mindful of moisture before watering. However, if you do encounter root rot, then you are going to need to be able to identify it.

There are two key ways to identify root rot—the first is to look at the roots that may or may not be rooting, and the second is to pay attention to the stem and the leaves of the plant. It might not always be an easy option to dig up your plant and check the roots, but if you grew the plant yourself, then chances are you will need to replant it in a new container at some point. When this time comes, check the roots. If there is no problem, you should see white or yellow roots, hopefully (but not always) with a fuzzy texture. Pulling a plant's roots out often destroys the fuzzy layer, but it will regrow as long as it is left alone to recover after replanting. But what about for sick roots?

Healthy roots are white or yellow; light brown roots are dried out and could use a drink. However, roots that are a dark brown color, and especially any roots that are black, are showing signs of root rot. Infected roots are many times slick and slimy, and generally feel gross to even touch. They also smell like rotting compost.

When you are replanting a succulent, this is a great time to check the roots to avoid planting a rotting plant in your garden. But this is also a painful experience for plants, so you mostly have to rely on the stem and the leaves of your succulents to tell you that something is wrong. The downside to this is that it really only tells you that your plants are dealing with the advanced stages of the disease. Starting near the bottom of the plant, leaves will start to lose their color and turn all mushy and gross. When this happens, the disease is too far gone to save the plant. You might get lucky and notice it early, but there isn't a whole lot that can usually be done when you've spotted it through the leaves. Keep in mind that root rot goes after the lower leaves first. Nutrient burn will also cause the leaves to lose their color, but it works its way down from the top of the plant.

Root rot is often too late to fix, but if you do manage to catch it early enough, then there will be some steps you can take. They won't necessarily save your plant, but they just might.

If root rot is being caused by overwatering, which is the most probable cause, then you might get really lucky and be able to save them by simply letting them dry. However, it needs to be caught *very* early for this to work. If the disease has moved into the stem or the leaves of the plant, the chances of it working are greatly reduced. This approach is best used for afflicted plants you caught while transplanting. Trimming away infected roots with some careful shear work may also save plants that have been caught at the root phase prior to rot entering the rest of the succulent.

For rot that has already gotten to the stem and the leaves, you are going to need to try saving the plant through propagation and growing it again. Succulents are great at propagating with a success rate of 4 out of 5. Meanwhile, they have only a 1 in 10 chance of surviving root rot that has spread into the leaves. Take your shears, cut off the top of the plant, and follow propagation steps to start regrowing the plant. You will have to get rid of the infected body of the plant and start growing it at a much smaller size again, but it is often the only way to treat your succulents.

Remember that the best way to prevent root rot is to keep an eye on it while you are transplanting seedlings and allow your plants to get plenty of dry time between waterings. If you can stay mindful of these two factors, then you might never have to deal with root rot affecting your succulents.

Pruning Your Succulents

There are many reasons you might want to prune your succulents. Thoughtful pruning can be done for health reasons, such as preventing rot. Pruning is most often done to promote and control new growth, and this can double to help promote healthy growth that will increase the life expectancy of your succulent. Just like with any plant, if you want them to look their best then you are going to have to give them some time and attention. Both indoor and outdoor succulents will need to be pruned, so it is best to learn how to make the process as smooth as possible, as it is a painful one for the plant if it isn't done properly.

As your succulent grows, the leaves closest to the soil will eventually start to lose their shape and consistency. They start to stop holding water and eventually they will just die. While this can be scary if you misdiagnose it as root rot, it is actually perfectly natural. The succulent has continued to grow new leaves, and these draw energy and attention away from the older ones. While these older leaves begin to die off, they are still taking up energy from the succulent, so pruning to remove these is a smart choice. This maintenance should be undertaken every couple weeks or so, but it doesn't need to have a tight schedule; just try to give the plant time to heal between sessions. Since the leaves you are removing are unhealthy and dead, you should be able to pull them away with your hands rather than rely on any tool. Make sure you have washed and dried your hands before doing so.

Another thing to keep an eye out for while thinking about removing dead leaves are leaves and other matter that has fallen off your plant or come in from some outside source, like other nearby plants. This matter will attract bugs and disease, so removing it as soon as you notice it is an important step in caring for your plants. While you need to give your succulents time to heal between removing dead leaves from it, you should check it every day to remove plant matter that has fallen off.

You can technically prune a succulent anytime you want, but most growers suggest doing so around the start of the growing season. This means that you will be pruning winter succulents in the fall, whereas summer succulents would be pruned in the spring. The reason for this is that pruning early in the growing season will leave plenty of time for you to see how your succulents are responding to the cuts. You should have a sharp pair of shears or scissors that can get through the stem in one quick cut. The fewer cuts it takes to prune your succulent, the better it will feel. When it comes to pruning properly, you should use a tool. Removing the dead leaves at the bottom doesn't require a tool, but proper pruning absolutely does, and a pair of shears or scissors will be the only necessary equipment you will need for pruning your succulents. That said, there are secondary tools that can make the experience much easier.

A tray of some sort that you can use to catch falling plant matter can make the pruning experience go by much quicker. You may also want a device for picking up material from plants without easy access; although if you've properly planned your succulent garden, then this shouldn't be a problem for you. If you are planning to also work in the soil, maybe plant some of your succulent clippings, then get your hands on a chopstick or similarly sized instrument to work the soil. Succulents don't require deep holes, so replanted cuttings don't require anything remotely as large as a shovel. With these tools, you can sit down to prune your plants however you like, but often, the best approach is to have a system in place so they can be sure every plant gets properly tended to. We'll follow an easy three-step process ourselves to behead, remove, and replant our succulents as necessary.

Beheading is done to keep your succulents in shape. When one of your succulents starts to grow too tall, you would carefully snip it quickly with your shears to remove the top and bring it down to the proper height. In this case, the proper height is whatever you choose it to be, based on the demands of the arrangement that you have created in your garden. When you snip off the top of your succulent, catch those pieces in your tray as you continue to work through the process. You won't be able to follow the replant step of the pruning process until you have a few of these tops. When you finish beheading and removing, bring these tops inside and let them dry for a minimum of one day. You should also be collecting any healthy looking leaves that have fallen off your succulent. These might also be able to work like cuttings to replant new succulents.

SUCCULENT GARDENING

Beheading is done to keep your plants in line, and it does have another effect. Cutting off the tops of plants typically causes them to start growing outwards. In similar fashion, pruning the sides tends to promote upward growth. Succulents tend to have a mind of their own when it comes to which direction they grow, thanks to their relationship to being planted closely together and the way they grow toward the sun. Keep all of this in mind when you make your cuts and watch how they react as they continue to grow. It is a good idea to try getting all of your pruning done at the same time. If you have a lot of succulents in your garden, then you may want to bring a notebook track those you've done already much easier. Another idea is to get some popsicle sticks and paint them two different colors. Take these with you as you prune your garden and stick a popsicle

SUCCULENT GARDENING

stick in the soil to note it has been pruned. Then, the next time you go to prune, all you need to do is take out the old popsicle stick and put the new color in. This quick method will take twenty minutes to paint and a bit more to dry, but it can last you years.

Just like how you remove dead leaves, you should remove dead plants wherever you encounter them. When you're out pruning, you should be checking in on each and every succulent you've planted, so it makes the perfect time to spot any that have passed on to the garden in the sky. At worst, it's a mini-tragedy in your garden. At best, it takes time and effort to pull them out. However, there is one positive to pulling a dead succulent out of your garden—you now have a space to plant the clippings and leaves that you collected in the first step. If you already have some dried out clippings and leaves, you can move right on to replanting. If not, then that's also okay; yank the dead plants out and call it a day.

Now for the fun part: replanting. Take those heads you cut off and stick them back in the soil. Cover them with a tiny bit of organic top soil to give them a little boost. This will help them to start developing roots and regrowing as a clone of the original plant. You can do this with the leaves as well, though don't be surprised if they prove to have a harder time taking off than the pieces you pruned yourself. Remember that the new cuttings need at least a day to dry. You can let them dry for longer, but you can't replant them before a day. Some growers recommend only working with cuttings that are perfectly straight. If there is a curve in the piece, they will cut it off. Try to remove the need to cut the plant twice by only removing straight pieces if you plan to replant them.

The best way to follow this three step process is to do it over two days. On the first day, prune all of your plants to behead those that need them. While doing this, also pay heed to step two and remove any dead plants you come across. On the second day, take those dried cuttings out and replant them in the spaces that have freed up. Day one and day two don't necessarily have to be next to each other; you can do it on two different weekends, for example. Just use your painted popsicle sticks to keep track of where the new plants are going.

Pest Control

For as long as there have been gardens, there have been pests. The battle between gardeners and pests has gone on since the dawn of time, and it will continue to go on until the end of time. It is a battlefield that has united countless generations of humans. The best thing to do is to try to avoid the battle for as long as possible. If you are an indoor gardener, you will have both your own unique benefits, along with unique challenges. Outdoor gardeners have less control over the environment, but this gives them a secret weapon that they can use. We'll start with the steps that indoor gardeners need to know, then we will look at some of the most frequently fought pests to see what can be done about them and learn more about that secret weapon.

Indoor Gardens: The best way to prevent pests or disease from attacking your indoor plants is to limit their access. If you are growing a garden in a room of its own, then you could create barriers and checks and balances to keep it clean quite easily. Putting up a mesh netting around the doorway can create a more secure environment. Make sure that there is a fan for airflow, both for the health of the plants and to make it more difficult for pests to land on them. Always remove dead plant matter and wash your hands before entering. Also, make sure there isn't a ton of dirt all over your clothing, as it could have harmful bacteria in it.

If you have your succulents spread out and about your home, then the chance of dealing with pests increases drastically. However, this does not mean that you necessarily will have them; it should merely be taken to mean you need to be a little more careful. Ensure that there is airflow where they are, but don't rely on an open window for it unless it has a screen. Even then, a fan is a better alternative if you are concerned about safety. Don't touch your plants with dirty hands, wash off any dirt from outdoors, and change into clean clothes if you are covered in mud or dirt. If you are careful about how you behave around your plants, you shouldn't have to deal with any of these pests, or at least have less of a chance of having to. Unfortunately, sometimes they show up even when you've been extremely careful. If that happens, chances are that you found yourself dealing with one of the following in the next section.

The Typical Villains

When it comes to pests, they really are just like the most annoying super villains. You can beat them one week and think they've disappeared, but then they're back again next time you look. If you're not careful about inspecting your plants, you could miss an infestation while it is still in the early stages and fairly easily defeatable. We'll look at some signs for early identification and prevention in a moment, but if you are going to see any pests on your succulents, it will probably be one of these sinister seven.

Ants: More than just the stars of their own movies, these little guys actually outnumber humans when it comes to population. This is because they can pretty much live in any environment. Some ant colonies can survive almost anywhere throughout the warmer seasons, and there are ants for almost every climate, which is all perfectly fine. If you see one or two ants, give them a nod and let them be; however, if you notice a whole bunch of them around your plants, then it is a likely sign of pest infestation. Ants aren't drawn to succulents naturally, but they are drawn to feed on pests that do. This will end up becoming both a sign that you have a pest problem, and likely a major one. Don't worry about ants when you see them, but do pay attention to and notice them before they become a problem.

Aphids: These guys are also remarkably small. They have little bodies shaped somewhat like a pear. They will most often be green, but there are also red, orange, and yellow aphids around, and you're likely to even spot other colors if you look long enough. They like to suck on the juices inside of your plant's leaves; these bites hurt your plants, and then they suck out the insides. Aphids are one of the creatures that ants like to feast on because aphids turn what they suck from your plants into honeydew. This waste product is packed full of sugar, so it is considered tasty to some species of insects. However, honeydew around your succulents can cause black mold to grow, eventually leading to plant death.

Fungus Gnats: If you are growing indoor plants, then the most likely villain you will encounter is the fungus gnat. These little guys can be mistaken for mosquitoes because they have little black bodies with two, almost-black wings and a little sucker-like face. They're a deadly combination of small and winged, allowing them to get into places that other pests would have a harder time reaching. If you are seeing a lot of fungus gnats, then this is a sign that you are overwatering

SUCCULENT GARDENING

your succulents and you need to slow down, as fungus gnats are most drawn toward soil that is nice and moist.

Mealybugs: When it comes to succulents grown outdoors, mealybugs are the most common pest. They're only a couple of millimeters long and come in an earthy brown shade. When they feed on your plants, they leave behind a weird "mealy" substance. This white residue looks almost like cotton or even maybe bland cotton candy. This isn't the only thing that mealybugs secrete, however; they release that same honeydew substance that aphids do, which means that, not only do they cover your plants in this weird substance, but they also put them at risk for mold infection. Mealybugs are a pain because once they take a foothold on a plant, they are quick to move on and attack those nearby, which can lead to entire beds in your garden becoming weak and sick.

Scale: Scale would be a really cool pest if it wasn't for the fact that it likes to attack our plants. This pest comes in all sorts of different varieties of shapes and shades, and succulents are especially delicious to armored scale and soft scale alike. You can spot these guys because they look like disgusting bumps in the leaves of your plants. They like to eat the sap from inside of the succulent leaves and they dig their way around in there. Doing this leaves a trail on the leaves that shows where the scale first entered and where it is now. These guys can quickly kill off the leaves of a succulent plant in no time at all.

Spider Mites: While these little guys aren't actually spiders, they are still super annoying. A spider would help catch bugs and prevent them from harming your plant, but spider mites are little red suckers that hang out on your plants and suck the juices out of them. They're very small and can be hard to spot, especially since they enjoy hiding on the bottom of leaves to avoid detection. The leaves of an infected plant will start to lose its fullness and its color. Be careful, as spider mites can kill off a plant very quickly, and they move from one to the next just as fast. Keep an eye out for webbing on your plants, as this can be an early sign that you have some spider mites to deal with.

Whiteflies: Whiteflies look almost like white rice. If you see little white flecks walking across your succulents, frequently jumping off them to flap their little white wings a couple times before landing back down, then you know you got a problem with whiteflies. They like succulents with leaves more than ones that look similar to cacti. They breed like rabbits too, making them a major hassle that needs to be treated the second they are detected. Whiteflies are another pest that both enjoys hiding on the bottom of leaves and leaving behind honeydew, thus opening up your succulents to the risk of disease.

Treating Your Succulents

The first step when it comes to treatment is to begin with prevention. You can't 100% prevent pests from your plants and go mad trying, but even the best setup could eventually have you dealing with something. The goal in prevention is simply to reduce the frequency of attack, and the two ways that this is done are also very important for the health of your plants in general.

The first step in prevention is to avoid overwatering your succulents. By this point in the book, you should already know that you should be doing this, but we are going to reemphasize it here because it poses yet another danger to your succulents. The second step is to ensure that there is good airflow on your plants. When you are indoors, this can easily be done with a fan, whereas outdoor gardeners are going to have to rely on the wind. Some steps you can take to help the wind out is to remove obstructions that are in the way between the wind source and your succulents. Keep in mind that there are various pros and cons to certain winds: overly strong winds can also tug newly planted succulents out of the ground, whereas strong airflow will make it harder for smaller pests to successfully land and stick to your plants.

A step that you can take specifically to prevent pests is to dissolve some neem oil into a water concentration and regularly spray your succulents with it on a weekly or bi-weekly basis. Neem oil is a combination of a few natural substances that insects dislike. Neem oil can be used as a part of a treatment for infestation, but it also makes a good part of any preventative routines you make to keep your succulents healthy. When using neem oil, it is best to apply it as the last thing you do during the day. This is because neem oil will make your succulents burn quicker, so apply it at times when they're in the shade or as the sun is going down.

Neem oil is a good part of a treatment system as well; however, you should also get your hands on some rubbing alcohol and dilute it with some water. Use this mixture by spraying it onto the infected plants to start killing off the pests. For pests like scales or mealybugs that leave behind a gross residue, you can put rubbing alcohol directly onto the damage to kill it off. This is best done with a cotton swab of some sort, so you can be direct and precise with your application. The spray bottle solution is for killing off and repealing the pests themselves.

Pests like ants and whiteflies are best treated with water. Blasting them off your succulents will knock them away and make it hard for them to get back to your plants, but be careful with this approach, as you don't want to accidentally overwater your succulents. Try to aim the water at the plant and away horizontally, or you may even consider laying down a tarp or something around the base of the plant to reduce how much water gets into the soil.

SUCCULENT GARDENING

You can always use a pesticide or insecticide if the problem gets too bad, but an organic solution should always be the first thing you try. These chemicals get into the ground and can really mess up the quality of the soil and destroy ecosystems you hadn't even realized were living down there. It can be a good idea to behead an infest succulent, remove the infected plant, and try growing it again. This can be a time consuming project, but it will be healthier for your garden.

Of course, if you are growing your succulents outside, then you have a secret weapon you can use to help protect your plants. You can release insects of your own into your garden. It might seem like a weird idea to go out and purchase bugs to add to your garden, but insects like ladybugs feed on pests, often reducing an infestation to nothing in a couple days. Plus, ladybugs are far cuter bugs than any of the pests we've looked at. They have wings and will fly away to go find more food once they've run out of pests to eat, which makes them the outdoor gardener's secret weapon.

Keep an eye out for signs of infestation in your garden. Discolored leaves, brown bumps or bite marks, bugs flying around in large quantities can all be clear signs of infestation. If you want to get into the habit of checking for earlier signs, then make it a habit to rub some paper towel on the bottom of your succulent's leaves. If it comes back with little streaks of blood, then you have an infestation to tackle. Also, check the soil around the base of the succulent to see if there is anything growing in it, as many pests like to lay their babies down there. Doing this together with the treatments listed above will give you the upper hand in tackling any battles with pests you might face quickly.

SUCCULENT GARDENING

Chapter Summary

- Caring for your succulents is an important part of being a gardener. You don't just get to toss some seeds in the yard and then forget about it; it takes care to keep your plants as healthy as possible.

- When it comes to watering your plants, it is always better to err on the side of caution and let them be dry for longer periods than it is to water them too much. Too much watering will kill your plants, but too little can merely remind them of their natural conditions.

- It is a beginner mistake to grow succulents in containers without proper drainage holes or in soil mixed to retain moisture.

- Indoor succulents should only be watered once a week. Completely soak the container when watering and allow it to completely and totally dry out before you water them again. You can check if it is time to water again by sticking a finger two inches in the soil. If the soil sticks to your finger, then it is still too moist to water again. Plants in a plastic container can be lifted to check the weight. If it is heavier than normal, there is still water left to drain.

- A good way to be on the safe side is to allow the soil to stay dry for a couple days before watering again. Your plants will grow healthier as a result.

SUCCULENT GARDENING

- Outdoor succulents will need to be watered more or less often, depending on the temperature outside. Ensure that the soil is allowed to drain completely before watering.

- Too much watering creates a growing environment with excess moisture. This is the perfect growing conditions for root rot, which is one of the biggest enemies that succulents can face.

- Root rot is a term used to describe a whole range of diseases that all grow in moist conditions. There are two kinds of root rot to deal with: the kind that kills your plants immediately, and the type that gets your plant sick and kills it slowly.

- Root rot can come from pathological factors like bacteria, but gardens that are properly tended to shouldn't have to deal with this problem. Indoor gardens can always bake their potting mixture ahead of planting if the gardener is worried about pathological root rot.

- When you look at the roots of your succulent plants, they should be white or yellow. Light brown roots are dried out and need water. Dark brown and black roots are a sign of root rot and they will be slimy to the touch. These should be removed prior to repainting.

SUCCULENT GARDENING

- Looking at the roots of a succulent isn't always a choice, but since you see the roots whenever you are replanting, you should be mindful of and watch for root rot when transplanting seedlings and such.

- You can also spot root rot by the way the leaves of the plant are behaving and, chances are, if it has spread to the leaves, then it is already too late for your succulent.

- Succulents should be pruned during the start of the growing season, either in spring or in fall, depending on whether your succulents are winter or summer growers.

- Dead leaves at the bottom of your succulent are perfectly normal, though they should still be removed whenever spotted.

- Pruning is done to control the size and growth of your succulents. Use clean shears and try to make clean, thorough cuts, so you can prevent unnecessary stress to your plants.

- Behead your plants and save the cuttings so that they can dry off for a day.

- Remove any dead plants you encounter while pruning and make note of the new spaces you can plant fresh succulents in.

SUCCULENT GARDENING

- On another day, take your dried-out cuttings from inside and plant them back in the soil. Propagating your plants in this manner keeps your garden beautiful, healthy, and growing strongly.

- Indoor gardeners can avoid battling pests by being extra careful about what they bring into the grow area. Clean clothes, washed hands, proper airflow, and caution will all help reduce the likelihood of infestation.

- Outdoor growers don't have as many options to prevent pests, but proper watering will help reduce the chances. Beneficial insects like ladybugs can be added to a garden to eat pests.

- The most common pests that succulents attract are ants, aphids, fungus gnats, mealybugs, scales, spider mites, and whiteflies.

- Many pests leave behind a substance called honeydew, which attracts ants and can cause mold to start attacking your plants.

- Treat your plants with neem oil to help prevent pests. Check the soil around the base of your succulents, as well as the bottom of their leaves, to spot pests early.

- Rubbing alcohol that has been watered down in a spray bottle will help treat infection, and carefully

SUCCULENT GARDENING

applied rubbing alcohol can reduce the damage and kill harmful substances that pests leave behind.

In the next chapter, you will learn all sorts of fun facts about your succulents, like how they interact with winter, the various medical benefits that they provide, and which succulents can make for a delicious and nutritious meal.

CHAPTER SIX

FUN FACTS ABOUT SUCCULENTS

Succulents are really neat plants, and there are some really cool things about them that didn't really fit properly anywhere else in the book so far. Consider this chapter to be a last look at why succulents are so cool. You should now have everything you need to know to add them to your garden; this is just the cherry on top.

Succulents and Winter

Succulents are primarily thought of as loving warm and dry places. Cold and wet doesn't exactly sound like a time that succulents would enjoy. Of course, there are some succulents that grow during the winter but, in general, can succulents survive the winter? The answer is yes; although, they won't be anything special to look at. That said, the most appropriate answer is "they can" rather than "they will."

If you are growing your succulents outside in the ground, then you will want to base which type of succulent you plant by the climate that you have throughout the year. Since we're focusing on winter alone right now, the succulents that you can consider can be divided into either a *hardy* and a *soft* category. Plants that are hardy are able to survive below-freezing temperatures. They may still go dormant during the winter, but they can survive conditions like frost. Soft succulents, on the other hand, will die in below-freezing temperatures, and frost will cause them considerable damage.

If you are raising soft succulents, then you have two options to get them through the winter: the first is to grow them inside to begin with. If you are growing plants inside, then winter conditions shouldn't affect the environment that you provide them with. However, if you still want to grow your soft succulents outside, then you should grow them in a container. One option is to grow them in an above-ground container and make the container itself a part of your garden's aesthetic. If an above-ground container doesn't work, you can always bury a container under the soil of your garden beds. If you plant your soft succulents in a container this way, then you can easily dig up that container and bring your plants in for the winter.

Speaking of the dormancy that was mentioned above, there is a small range in which most succulents fall. There are succulents that continue to grow during the winter, succulents that go into a partially dormant phase, and then those that go completely dormant. The dormant phase doesn't require extra fertilizer. There are some species who go completely dormant by shedding their above ground foliage every year. Their root system stays healthy and alive in the soil, so when warmer weather comes, the succulent can start growing again.

SUCCULENT GARDENING

As winter approaches, there are three steps to follow for your hardy succulents. Anything that can be transplanted or brought inside should be brought in roughly a month before you expect frost to start being an issue. This is an optional step rather than a must since hardy plants can withstand winter. The second step is to keep up with your maintenance and remove any dead leaves, as the temperature and moisture of a winter environment will turn dead leaves into deadly factories of infectious bacteria and diseases. Finally, you should put in place some kind of waterproofing to reduce the damage it causes. Look for trees or other hanging objects that could drip water down on your succulents. A hardy succulent will stay alive under the snow, but one that is dealing with health issues will rot, which can introduce a biological contaminant into the ecosystem you grow your succulents.

Soft succulents are going to want to be brought indoors, as they will die outside.

Succulents Can Grow on Walls

One of the coolest things about succulents is that they can grow on surfaces that are completely vertical. Most plants need to be planted in the ground. Some of these can grow vines that can creep up a wall, but succulents can grow from the wall itself, so long as they are provided what they need.

SUCCULENT GARDENING

In order to grow succulents on a vertical surface best, you will need to select kinds that don't need much watering, as doing so will help them immensely. They still need some soil to set their roots, so this is best done in carefully controlled methods. One favorite is to take a picture frame and attach it to a tree or a fence. You can add your soil into the frame once it is attached, then plant a bunch of succulents in the soil. They will grow up and out of the picture frame, creating a cool 3D look and making for absolutely spellbinding decorations around your yard.

The picture frame approach is just one of many methods you can use. Another that has become more popular as of late is to bring a wall to life by covering it entirely in beautiful succulents. This is mostly done to

SUCCULENT GARDENING

barns or sheds. A wall of beautiful, colorful, and lively succulents is a beautiful thing. You can also grow a living wall using only succulents that have nutritional or health benefits, so then it becomes both beautiful and beneficial, making it the best kind of addition to your garden.

You Can Even Wear Succulents

Remember how we talked about the fact that succulents were becoming more fashionable thanks to the internet? Perhaps there is no greater proof of this fact than succulent jewelry. That's right—there is jewelry being made from succulents. You might think that somebody harvested one of the prettier varieties of succulent and used it to create a beautiful ring or earring, but succulent jewelry is so much cooler than that. One trend that hopefully increases in the coming years is jewelry made out of living succulents.

Succulents tend to be pretty hardy plants, which means they can survive some weird conditions for impressive amounts of time. The weirdest position that a succulent could find itself is attached to your wrist or wrapped around your finger, but people have been attaching succulents to jewelry and wearing them as a beautiful way to accessorize their outfits. If you grow your own succulents, then you can find guides on how to make these pieces yourself and really see the way it wows the people you show them off to.

Succulent jewelry is a cool way to combine gardening with another hands-on craft, and it can be a ton of fun for both adults and kids alike to make their own succulent pieces.

They Truly Do Come in All Colors

While the majority of the succulents that you would grow are probably going to be green, especially if you are an indoor grower, that doesn't mean there is any limitation on the colors that succulents come in. There is literally a succulent for every shade in the rainbow—and then some!

SUCCULENT GARDENING

As you continue to increase your ability to take care of succulents and you grow more comfortable in your skills, you will be able to start branching out into all sorts of different species of succulents and see for yourself that the color combinations they offer for arrangements are truly limitless. There are as many options for succulent patterns as there are for flowers, which is great for those gardeners who live in dry climates that don't flavor flowers as much. Succulents are more than able to provide the lively color your property needs.

SUCCULENT GARDENING

Chapter Summary

- Despite loving warm and dry conditions, some succulents can survive perfectly well when kept outdoors for the winter.

- Succulents can be categorized as soft or hardy. Soft succulents can't deal with the frost or below freezing temperatures, whereas hardy succulents can withstand the frost and keep themselves alive despite below freezing weather.

- Soft succulents should be raised indoors or in containers if outside. You can keep containers above ground for easy movement, or you can bury containers in the soil to hide their presence. Digging up containers and bringing soft succulents inside for the winter will help keep them alive.

- Most succulents go into a state of dormancy in the winter, though there are species that grow during the winter. If your succulents go into a dormant phase, then there is no need to continue watering and fertilizing them during the winter.

- Hardy succulents are still at risk from overly moist conditions. Make sure there is no water dripping on them as snow melts. They can stay alive under a snow bank if they are healthy, but ones that are unhealthy will die off in the winter weather.

SUCCULENT GARDENING

- Succulents can be grown vertically to create really cool ornaments for your walls, trees, or fences. It is surprisingly easy to pull off these cool vertical gardens, though you should have some experience with growing succulents before you try this.

- One cool use for succulents are to attach living plants to jewelry and wear them as part of a fancy dress. It's a cool look and one that not many plants can withstand.

- Succulents come in every color of the rainbow, and they survive in conditions that many other plants can't. This makes succulents a fantastic choice for your gardening needs.

FINAL WORDS

You now have everything you need to start planting and taking care of your very own beautiful and colorful succulent garden. Whether it is indoors or outdoors, you know all the steps necessary to prepare to start growing a new species and keep it healthy throughout its life cycle.

The first step to growing any succulent is to do your research. Before buying containers and starting seeds, research is necessary to ensure that you understand what the species you have chosen requires. This research is done simply by asking somebody at your local garden center or searching online. It shouldn't take more than ten or twenty minutes, but it will let you know exactly what you need to provide for your specific plant. It can also tell you whether or not you are capable of raising that particular succulent. If you are, then you know exactly what to do.

Careful attention must be paid to how much you water your plants, and you should know exactly why that is now. Thanks to the knowledge in this book, you should be able to avoid issues like root rot for years if you are careful. You also know what you need to do to prevent pests from snacking on your succulents and where to grow them to prevent infestation, infection, sunburn, and drowning. It is this knowledge that is going to keep your succulents safe and healthy in your garden because you know better than to make beginner mistakes, like leaving your succulents growing in direct sunlight throughout the day.

Remember that the more colorful a succulent is, the more likely that it will be harder to grow that particular succulent. Those succulents that produce flowers throughout the year will be among the hardest to grow and maintain. Also difficult will be succulents that require entirely different environmental needs than those of your local climate. These succulents will need to be grown either inside your house or in a greenhouse, in which the environment can be controlled. This can be a very rewarding experience, but it also demands more of the gardener than a beginner should worry about just yet. However, if you put into practice the knowledge you've learned from this book, then you are well on your way past beginner, and you will be ready for harder challenges in no time.

www.ingramcontent.com/pod-product-compliance
Lightning Source LLC
Chambersburg PA
CBHW050323120526
44592CB00014B/2028